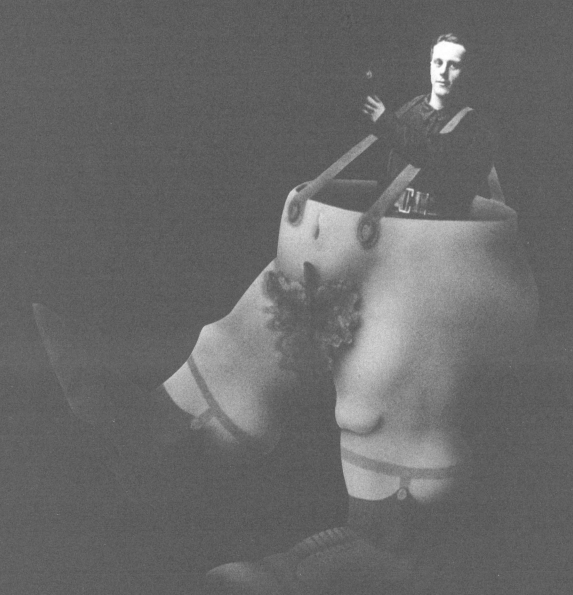

THIS IS A CARLTON BOOK

First published in Great Britain in by Carlton Books Ltd
An imprint of the Carlton Publishing Group
20 Mortimer Street
London W1T 3JW

Editorial: Ross Hamilton
Design: Russell Knowles
Production: Rachel Burgess

A CIP catalogue for this book is available from the British
Library.

ISBN 978-1-78739-321-9

Printed in Dubai

10 9 8 7 6 5 4 3 2 1

ACKNOWLEDGEMENTS:
The publishers would like to thank Holly Gilliam for her
invaluable contribution.

PHOTOGRAPHS:
Bruce Cole; Sam Emerson; Jill Furmanovsky; Steve Morley;
Michael Putland; Martha Swope; The New York Times;
Barrie Wentzell; Python (Monty) Pictures Limited

Script extracts on pages 22, 23, 24, 26, 27, 28, 30, 32,
66, 67, 68, 70, 71, 72, 88, 89, 91, 93 from Monty Python's
Flying Circus Just the Words Volume 1 by Monty Python
(Methuen) and Monty Python's Flying Circus Just the Words
Volume 2 by Monty Python (Methuen), reprinted courtesy of
Methuen Publishing.

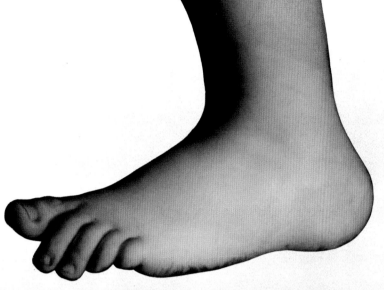

Monty Python's FLYING CIRCUS

50 years of hidden treasures

Adrian Besley

CARLTON BOOKS

Monty Python's FLYING CIRCUS

TIMELINE

- General stuff
- Live Stuff
- Music Things
- Film Bits

1939: John Cleese born October 27

1940: Terry Gilliam born November 22

1941: Graham Chapman born January 8

1942: Terry Jones born February 1

1943: Eric Idle born 29 March

1943: Michael Palin born May 5

1969: Monty Python's Flying Circus first broadcast

1970: Monty Python's Flying Circus

1971: The Lanchester Arts Festival, Coventry. Three midnight shows at the Coventry Arts Theatre

1971: *And Now For Something Completely Different*

1971: *Another Monty Python Record*

1972: *Monty Python's Previous Record*

1973: April 27–May 24: Monty Python's First Farewell Tour. 30 shows in 13 cities around the UK

1973 Summer: Monty Python's First Farewell Tour of Canada. From Toronto to Vancouver

1973: *The Monty Python Matching Tie and Handkerchief*

October 1974: The first broadcast of Monty Python's Flying Circus in the USA

1974 March: Monty Python Live at Drury Lane! two–week run, extended to four at London's Royal Theatre

1974: Monty Python Live at Drury Lane

1975: The Album of the Soundtrack of the Trailer of the Film of Monty Python and the Holy Grail

1975: *Monty Python and the Holy Grail*

1939 1940 1941 1942 1943 1969 1970 1971 1972 1973 1974 1975

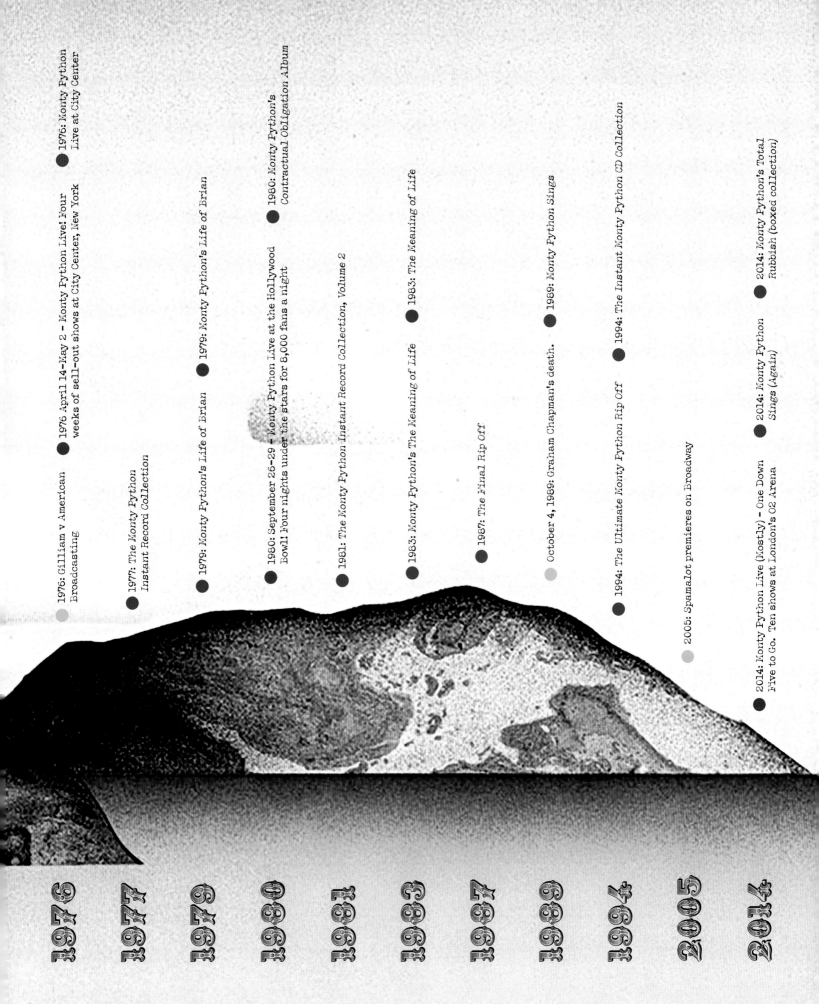

1976: Gillian v American Broadcasting

1976 April 14–May 2 – Monty Python Live! Four weeks of sell-out shows at City Center, New York

1976: Monty Python Live at City Center

1977: *The Monty Python Instant Record Collection*

1979: *Monty Python's Life of Brian*

1979: *Monty Python's Life of Brian*

1980: September 26–29 – Monty Python Live at the Hollywood Bowl! Four nights under the stars for 8,000 fans a night

1980: *Monty Python's Contractual Obligation Album*

1981: *The Monty Python Instant Record Collection, Volume 2*

1983: *Monty Python's The Meaning of Life*

1983: *The Meaning of Life*

1987: *The Final Rip Off*

1989: *Monty Python Sings*

October 4, 1989: Graham Chapman's death.

1994: *The Ultimate Monty Python Rip Off*

1994: *The Instant Monty Python CD Collection*

2005: Spamalot premieres on Broadway

2014: Monty Python Live (Mostly) – One Down Five to Go. Ten shows at London's O2 Arena

2014: *Monty Python Sings (Again)*

2014: *Monty Python's Total Rubbish* (boxed collection)

1976
1977
1979
1980
1981
1983
1987
1989
1994
2005
2014

Foreword by the Pythons

-----------------------original message------------- ----

From: John Cleese@mp.com
Sent: Thursday, May 19, 2016, 3:05
Subject: Foreword

I am very flattered, indeed humbled, to be asked to write this forward for the famous Monty Python group.

And I'm absolutely delighted to do so.

John Cleese

Carlton, the publishers of what they feel is one of the most original and fascinating books ever produced by Monty Python have asked us to let you all know that this is one of the most original and fascinating books ever produced by the Monty Python team. We must emphasise that they asked us in a very nice way. Reports that Terry Gilliam was water-boarded are ludicrous and exaggerated. He was having a bath anyway. Similarly any charge that Eric Idle was paid half a million Zambian kwacha to endorse the book is quite without foundation, and before anyone accuses him of laundering anything apart from the occasional shirt, they should realise that the exchange rate is 14,687 kwacha to the pound, making Eric's non-existent inducement worth little more than £6,000, which even if it had been made available to him, is precious little for a foreword, in today's market conditions.

It's worth making the point that the Python team have always supported their product wherever possible, and it is a very rare thing indeed that the writing of this foreword coincided with John Cleese's first-ever total blackout and Michael Palin's filming of his new series "Twenty Thousand Leagues Beneath the Sea", which requires him to be in a bathyscape for eight weeks with only limited email access. Terry Jones was, as ever, keen to take on the task himself, but his insistence that he be rewarded with a vineyard, rather than the traditional bottle of wine, was just too much for a publisher in these difficult times.

Thank goodness for Graham Chapman, who though he is still appealing against being sent to Heaven by mistake, stepped into the breach and found time to dictate this foreword to Mrs Elsie Griffiths, a medium from Margate.

PissOff!!
Love - Monty Python

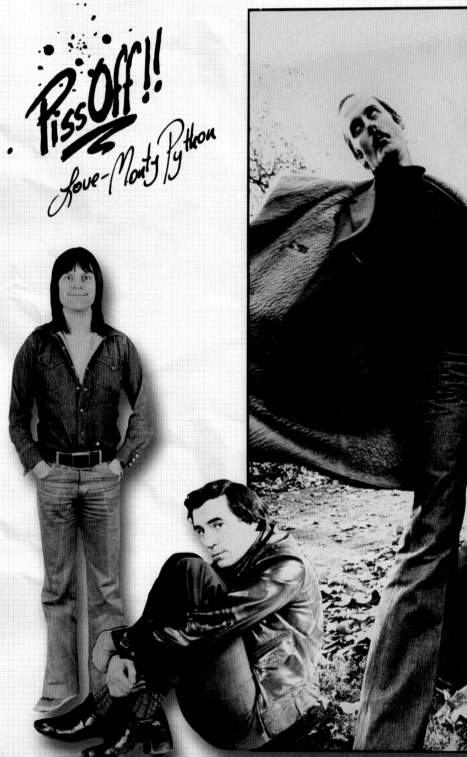

I have been asked by … I'm sorry I forget who … to write about er … I'm sorry I forget what. Oh, that's right, it's a book. And a very good one. The binding is fabulous, the paper well chosen, and even the ink is very safe for the environment. As to the people it describes they seem fascinating, and awfully clever. I wonder why I have never heard of them. But of course it was all a long time ago, and they do seem to have been rather successful with whatever it was they did back then. I have no hesitation whatever in recommending this book as one of the finest bits of fiction I have ever read. Social history? That's right, sorry, one of the finest Part Two's of the social history of some of the greatest anti-social people who ever existed. I can put my hand on my heart transplant and say without fear or favour that if you read this book you will have done very well. I commend er … the Publishers, whoever they be, on such a splendid job. A book on cricket is just what we all needed.

Eric Idle
The Old Jokes Home
Surbiton

A Foreword by Graham Chapman

"Hello, are you there?"
 "Yes I am here"
"What is your name?"
 "Graham Champion"
"Do you mean Chapman?"
 "Yes, I do, sorry"
"Graham, do you have any message for the book-buying public?"
 "Yes I do"
"What is it?"
 "This is my message and what it is too."
(pause)
"Go on"
 "My message to the book-buying public is this."
"Yes?"
 "That this is a very good book. It recounts the story of all six members, from early days in the Cambridge Footlights and farther afield, through early appearances on the BBC, global stardom, movie-making, fights re-unions, and death, to the final curtain drop in London's 02 Arena in July 2014. The "treasures " are reloadable facsimiles of priceless artefacts from the official Python archives and include..."
(pause)
"I've lost you Graham"
(long pause)
"Graham, are you there?
 (Another voice) "Hello, I'm God. Graham's gone to the toilet. I haven't had time to read the book myself but it does seem to be a very good book. It recounts the story of all six-"
"Sorry, God. I hate to interrupt, but we've had that bit. Can you tell us a bit more about the priceless artefacts?
"Yes, I certainly can. They include hand-annotated scripts, rare photographs, posters, programmes and tickets from classic shows, original items of animation artwork and many more."
"Thank you. Can we say God recommends it?"
"Absolutely"
"Thank You. This is a dream come true for us here at the publishers."
"Certainly the best thing I've read since Fifty Shades of Gay"
"Can we edit that last bit?"

INTRO-DUCTION

IN JULY 2014, FIVE SEPTUAGENARIAN COMEDIANS WITH A COMBINED AGE OF 357, PLUS GRAHAM CHAPMAN ON SCREEN, PERFORMED A LIVE SHOW OVER TEN NIGHTS TO MORE THAN 150,000 PEOPLE. THE FINAL PERFORMANCE WAS BROADCAST IN THEATRES IN MORE THAN 100 COUNTRIES. NOT BAD FOR A COMEDY GROUP WHO HAD NOT PERFORMED TOGETHER FOR OVER 30 YEARS…

Many have noted that in the Autumn of 1969, just as the Pythons were putting together ideas for the first series of *Monty Python's Flying Circus*, another seminal group, The Beatles, were on the brink of dissolution. George Harrison, the most devoted celebrity fan of the "Pythons", believed the spirit of the Fab Four continued in the Surreal Six. In terms of originality, creativity and popularity, he certainly had a point.

The phenomenon that is Monty Python is more akin to a rock band than anything television or theatre can supply. They perform together as a group, but wrote their greatest work alone or in partnership; fans greet the opening of sketches just like the first few bars of a favourite song and, like so many bands, they have partied, bickered, even tragically lost a group member, but retained a brotherly spirit that ultimately keeps the group alive across the years.

Like their pop-music forerunners, Monty Python are now a cultural monument. The word 'Pythonesque' is listed in the *Oxford English Dictionary* ("After the style or resembling the absurdist, the surrealist humour of *Monty Python's Flying Circus*"); their most famous sketch (and now an established meme) "Dead Parrot" was referenced in a speech by British Prime Minister Margaret Thatcher, and the language used every day by computer programmers (who also co-opted the term 'spam' from the sketch), as well as asteroids, fossils, a Ben and Jerry's ice cream and even an endangered woolly lemur, have all been named in their honour.

In an unmarked room of a high-security storage facility in London lie the boxes, files and tapes of the Monty Python archive. Here is the documentation that details half a century of comedy history and within it lie some incredible treasures. With exclusive access to this fascinating collection, this book replicates some of those rarely seen documents in a celebration of the 45 episodes of *Monty Python's Flying Circus* (as well as two Bavarian special episodes) and their afterlife in the live shows that established and then punctuated the careers of six incredible individuals.

Adrian Besley, London, 2016

LIFE BEFORE PYTHON

THERE WAS NO 'BIG BANG'. MONTY PYTHON DIDN'T JUST HAPPEN. THE SIX MEMBERS WHO WOULD BE BOUND TOGETHER FOR THE REST OF THEIR LIVES WERE ALREADY BUILDING CAREERS IN TV COMEDY WHEN THE OPPORTUNITY TO DO 'SOMETHING COMPLETELY DIFFERENT' AROSE...

The Pythons came together in the Swinging 60s, when the UK had finally shaken off its grey, post-war mood, loosened its collar and broadened its horizons. Comedy had also broken its shackles. Spike Milligan was bringing the anarchic hilarity of *The Goons* to TV, while Oxbridge graduates, including Peter Cook and David Frost, had established satire as a comedy vehicle in *Not Only... But Also* and *That Was the Week That Was*.

At Cambridge University in the early 60s, John Cleese, Graham Chapman and Eric Idle had successfully written and performed sketches in the Footlights theatrical club, while around the same time, Michael Palin and Terry Jones were treading a similar path in Oxford University's Revue Group. However, as students of Britain's

elite universities they were preparing for a life in law, medicine or academia. Comedy was surely a bit of light relief from their studying – wasn't it?

The blossoming of sketch-based comedy in the cabaret clubs of London, the theatrical success of *Beyond the Fringe* and the expansion of television as ITV's franchises multiplied and BBC2 was launched, all provided opportunities for new comedy. Moreover, through Peter Cook, David Frost, Jonathan Miller, Alan Bennett and producers such as Humphrey Barclay, Oxbridge had established a strong foothold in TV – the future Pythons were stepping into fertile ground...

Below: John Cleese joined Ronnie Corbett on *The Frost Report*. Pythons-to-be would also contibute to the writing.

Above: *Help!*, issue number 24, May 1965. Gilliam met Cleese while working on the magazine.

A DIFFERENT CIRCUS

John Cleese was the first to test the waters. Footlights' 1963 revue, *A Clump of Plinths* (later retitled *Cambridge Circus*) had been a hit at the Edinburgh Fringe Festival, taken London's West End by storm and enjoyed a stint on Broadway. John was one of the show's stand-out writers and performers, while Graham Chapman was enticed onto the show, deferring his studies at a London hospital. As he picked up jobs writing for Roy Hudd, Petula Clark and Cilla Black, Graham's career as a doctor was put on hold.

Above: The cast of *The Frost Report*. **Below left:** A flyer for the Oxford Revue, including Palin and Jones. **Below right:** Graham Chapman appears alongside Tim Brooke-Taylor.

> **"CAMBRIDGE CIRCUS, LIKE ALL THE INTIMATE REVUES OF RECENT VINTAGE, HAS BEEN WRITTEN LARGELY BY ITS CAST. THREE OF THE NUMBERS—THE OPENING, CLOSE AND A SPOOF OF WEST SIDE STORY CALLED WEST END SAGA—ARE CREDITED TO SOMEONE CALLED CARDINAL RICHELIEU."**
> **NEW YORK TIMES, 1964**

John Cleese extended his stay in New York, joining the cast of Tommy Steele's *Half a Sixpence* before venturing to Chicago for a short-lived journalistic stint at *Newsweek*. By the time he returned to London in 1964, *Cambridge Circus* had morphed into the BBC Radio series *I'm Sorry, I'll Read That Again*. Cleese was able to return to the show and link up with both Chapman and Eric Idle, who was by now a regular contributor, too.

On the other side of the world, a young Terry

Gilliam had progressed through Occidental College in Los Angeles and was working in an ad agency. The humour and visual techniques he had developed at the college paper provided his means of escape. He secured work in New York with *Mad* magazine editor Harvey Kurtzman's new venture, a humour magazine called *Help!*. It was working on this magazine that Gilliam, seeking a model for a photographic comic strip, approached a young Englishman who was appearing in a Broadway show – John Cleese.

By 1966, Jones and Palin had both taken a tentative step into television. Jones had secured a £20-a-week salaried post as a comedy script advisor at the BBC, while Palin had a brief stint as an anchorman on a Bristol-based pop show called *Now*. Soon they were back working together, performing at cabaret clubs, writing filmed sketches for *The Late Show* and penning links for the likes of Russ Conway and Ken Dodd.

FROSTY RECEPTION

If the future Pythons needed inspiration, they only had to look to the high-achieving David Frost. A former Footlights star just a few years their senior, Frost had catapulted to stardom in 1962 with *That Was the Week That Was*. Having kept a close eye on the young guns of comedy, Frost was ready to unleash them – alongside a few old hands – in 1966's *The Frost Report*. The show would feature Ronnie Barker, Ronnie Corbett and John Cleese,

with a writing roster that included not only Bill Oddie, Tim Brooke-Taylor and Marty Feldman, but also Chapman, Cleese, Idle, Jones and Palin.

The Frost Report focused on a different theme each week. Anchored by Frost himself, the show featured live songs and sketches, and Jones/Palin-written filmed inserts. While Eric Idle specialised in monologues and Cleese/Chapman supplied sketches, all three would provide Frost's witty chat. This was known as Continuing Developing Monologue (CDM) which they referred to as Cadbury's Dairy Milk or OJATIL (Old Jokes and Totally Irrelevant Links).

While the Pythons didn't write the most famous *Frost Report* sketch, *The Class System* ("I look down on him because…"), the show's satirical bent meant ridiculing authority figures and the ludicrousness of the class system, as typified in Palin/Jones's *Judges at Recess* sketch. These were themes that would be replayed in many *Flying Circus* sketches. Just as importantly, the show introduced the Pythons to the discipline of attending team meetings to discuss and read out their material to fellow writers.

The Frost Report was a resounding success, garnering critical acclaim and viewing figures that grew from 2.5 to 12 million in six weeks. And, when the show won the 1967 Golden Rose of Montreux (the first British winner since *The Black and White Minstrel Show*!), it brought the young writers more welcome attention.

"TO BE 23 AND ON THE FROST REPORT WAS PRETTY COOL." ERIC IDLE

With *The Frost Report* running its course after 13 episodes, the entrepreneurial Frost set up his own TV company, Redifusion, and offered his stars Cleese and Brooke-Taylor a new show. In turn, they co-opted Chapman and Feldman, and *At Last the 1948 Show* (a joke on how long it took TV commissioners to actually make a decision) was born. With the satire boom finally subsiding, the writers were now off the leash and able to push their sillier, cheekier comedy to the fore.

"WE AVIDLY WATCHED THE '48 SHOW BECAUSE THAT WAS THE FUNNIEST, FRESHEST THING AROUND." TERRY JONES

There is much in *The '48 Show* that is familiar to the Python fan. Sketches featured a silly walking doctor, a patient with too-thin legs and a man walking into a shop, looking to buy some chartered accountants. There are TV spoofs on vox pops, news readers and even a continuity announcer ('the

THE OXFORD REVUE GROUP

Michael Palin   Mike Wyn Jones

Robert Hewison   Terry Jones

David Peacock

will be appearing in Cabaret

every night from 1 to 6 June

in

the new Coq au Vin Grill Room of

THE GREAT WESTERN HOTEL

NEWQUAY

Above: Issue 24 of *Help!* magazine included the (fictional) story "Christopher's Punctured Romance", starring John Cleese.

Right: From the pages of *Varsity*, a cartoon of the Footlights Revue of 1963, including future Pythons John Cleese and Graham Chapman.

Far right: A ticket for filming of *The Complete and Utter History of Britain*, created and written by Terry Jones and Michael Palin.

LEFT TO RIGHT: Bill Oddie, John Cleese, David Hatch, Jo Kendall, Graham Chapman, Jonathan Lynn, Tim Brooke-Taylor.

This is a drawing (made especially for this celebration edition of Varsity) of the London-New York cast of "Cambridge Circus" by their director Humphrey Barclay. This was the record-breaking Footlights Revue of 1963, which spawned a group of comedians who have made an enormous mark on the entertainment scene since then. Between them they have created BBC Radio's "I'm Sorry, I'll Read That Again", BBC TV's "Twice A Fortnight", and Rediffusion's "At Last The 1948 Show" and "Do Not Adjust Your Set", four comedy shows which have broken completely new ground. Humphrey Barclay used to draw for Varsity and is now a TV producer (with Rediffusion).

EIGHTPENCE

LONDON Oct 7-Oct 13

TV TIMES

COVER :
Tim Brooke-Taylor
John Cleese
Aimi Macdonald
Graham Chapman
Marty Feldman . . .

AT LAST THE 1948 SHOW
Tuesday, 8-45 p.m.

THE FROST PHILOSOPHY
pages 16-17

Champion jockey **JOSH GIFFORD** looks at the new NATIONAL HUNT SEASON pages 2-3

lovely' Aimi MacDonald) who says "and now for something completely different".

Some sketches would re-appear in later Python shows and Amnesty International benefits. These included Graham Chapman's one-man wrestling bout, the *Beekeeper* and *Bookshop* sketches, and, most famously, *Four Yorkshireman* – always a crowd favourite at live Python shows.

NOT ADUSTING

1967 was also turning out to be a busy year for Michael Palin and Terry Jones. They had been writing and performing their own filmed sketches on BBC's *The Late Show*, contributing to John Bird and John Fortune's *A Series of Birds* and appearing on *Twice a Fortnight*, a sketch show also featuring Bill Oddie, Graeme Garden and, future *Yes Minister* co-writer, Jonathan Lynn.

By the end of the year, they were reunited with Eric Idle for their very own series, with actors David Jason and Denise Coffey. *Do Not Adjust Your Set* was ostensibly a children's show, but, with the inclusion of surreal musical group, The Bonzo Dog Doo-Dah Band, it soon found itself attracting a young adult following. Jones, Palin and Idle were now all on screen, performing proto-Python items like the *Going For A Song* (TV antiques show) parody, shopkeeper sketches and "naked" links.

"GRAHAM AND I WOULD FINISH EARLY ON A THURSDAY TO WATCH DO NOT ADJUST YOUR SET. IT WAS THE FUNNIEST THING ON TELEVISION." JOHN CLEESE

An undoubted hit, *Do Not Adjust Your Set* went to a second series, by which time Palin and Jones were also working on *The Complete and Utter History of Britain* for London Weekend Television. This took a now obviously Pythonesque look into the annals, using mock adverts, sports commentary, news reports, film trailers and other soon-to-be familiar devices.

Meanwhile, Terry Gilliam had found himself in London and, on the advice of his old acquaintance John Cleese, presented *Do Not Adjust Your Set* producer, Humphrey Barclay, with some sketches and cartoons. Barclay introduced him to a welcoming Idle and a slightly more reticent Jones and Palin, and encouraged the American to contribute animated shorts. It only took his *Christmas Card* and the stream-of-consciousness *Elephants* to win his future colleagues around. Later in the year, Barclay would find Gilliam more TV work as "resident cartoonist" alongside Eric Idle on Frank Muir's *We Have Ways of Making You Laugh*.

By the late 60s, the future Pythons were increasingly working together. Shows like Ronnie Corbett's *That's Me Over Here*, Feldman's *Marty* and BBC 2's *Broaden Your Mind* had involved various combinations of the writers. The one-off show for the US, called *How to Irritate People*, featured Chapman, Cleese and Palin, and included *Job Interview* and other sketches, which would re-appear in some form in subsequent series of *Flying Circus*. They were all well aware of each other's talents, it just needed destiny, serendipity or a programme opportunity to bring them together…

Opposite: The *TV Times* from October 1967. The show ran from 1967–68 and, according to Wikipedia, was credited with bringing "Cambridge Footlights humour to a broader audience".

Below: An early Terry Gilliam Christmas Card. This may be used freely upon sending £15 (€400) in an envelope to the address on page 67.

London Weekend Television invites you on Thursday 21st. November 1968 to **THE COMPLETE AND UTTER HISTORY OF BRITAIN** (IN SEVEN BITS) by Michael Palin and Terry Jones

ADMIT ONE

Children under 15 years not admitted

Wembley Studios, Empire Way, Wembley from 8.00-9.30 p.m. Doors Open 7.30-7.45 p.m.

Merry Christmas!

ILLUSTRATED BY TERRY GILLIAM

THE COMING TOGETHER

LIKE ALL CREATION STORIES, THERE ARE SEVERAL VERSIONS IN CIRCULATION, BUT RECEIVED WISDOM SUGGESTS THE MOMENT OF GENESIS CAME WHEN JOHN CALLED MICHAEL TO SAY, "I'VE SEEN THE COMPLETE AND UTTER HISTORY… YOU WON'T BE DOING ANY MORE OF THOSE, WILL YOU?" AND FLOATED THE IDEA OF DOING A SHOW TOGETHER.

Palin, Jones and Idle already had an offer on the table from Thames TV to make a grown-up *Do Not Adjust Your Set*, but had been told they would have to wait over a year for a free studio. Cleese had been offered a solo show, but was more inclined to work with others, especially Palin. The DNAYS gang were initially cautious, but within a couple of weeks had seen the opportunity and potential adventure in the proposal.

Eschewing the attentions of David Frost, who wanted the show for his Paradine Productions, the new group were taken under the wing of BBC comedy consultant, Barry Took. He hosted some exploratory meetings with them before strongly encouraging BBC Head of Comedy, Michael Mills, to sign them up. Mills supposedly baulked at being told what to do by a mere comedy writer, and compared Took to Baron Van Richthofen (German fighter pilot, AKA the Red Baron) and his Flying Circus. Internally, the BBC subsequently referred to the

project as *Baron Von Took's Flying Circus*.

The Pythons remember their first meeting with Mills as a complete shambles. The six, including Terry Gilliam, whose involvement was assumed but not clarified, appeared to have no idea what their show would be like. What's it going to be about? Are you using film? Is there to be music? Will there be

guest stars? The answer to all these questions was essentially, "Er… we don't know." However, to their surprise, Mills announced, "I'll give you 13 episodes, you're on air in October, but that's all I can give you. Now go away and get on with it." That was it. No pilot, no definite structure and no name, but the show was up and running.

"Only then would the BBC have taken such a risk on a totally unknown group. I was the only one who was a recognisable performer at that time." John Cleese

PUSHING THE BOUNDARIES

The spring of 1969 was an exciting time to be a (still un-christened) Python as they ticked off the wish list for their own series. They wanted to extend existing sketch-show comedy; not be constrained by what was ridiculous or even incomprehensible to a mass audience. (Cleese recalled how a sketch was rejected for *The 1948 Show* with, 'Very funny, boys, but they won't get it in Bradford.'). They wanted to do away with the need for a punchline and play around with conventions. And they wanted artistic control; to have their scripts performed as they had written them, in the right locations with a director sympathetic to their aims.

Then they saw Spike Milligan's new series *Q5*. It was as if the ex-Goon had stolen their wish list. Jones remembers phoning Cleese after watching it and saying, "Isn't that what we are meant to be doing?" However, rather than be discouraged by Milligan's pioneering, free-flowing, anarchic style, they were emboldened and inspired to take things even further.

A breakthrough came when Jones remembered 'Elephants', the stream-of-consciousness animation Gilliam had made for DNAYS. The new show could use the animations to link from one sketch to another. Once they agreed on this structure, free from the need to write punchlines or even endings to sketches, they felt liberated in the way they could write.

The team's working patterns were established at the outset. They would meet at one or other's homes or at a favourite curry house and discuss ideas for the show. They would separate and write – Cleese and Chapman mainly penning studio sketches, Palin and Jones largely working on their location-shot pieces and Idle working alone on his monologues and skits. Then, two weeks later, they would meet again to read, amend and evaluate the material, and decide what would go into each show.

Meanwhile, Terry Gilliam would be frantically cutting out and assembling his animations on a shoestring budget. He would attend the read-through meetings, where his opinion on the proposed content was valued, but his attempts to describe his still-unmade animations often left the others bemused. He did, however, discover which sketches he would be required to link.

The read-throughs were the hub of the operation. Cleese and Palin read out their respective pair's output and Idle read out his. Some sketches were instantly and unanimously approved, some were discarded and some were earmarked for amendments and rethinks, even

> **"The writers were in charge. That was so unique then. There were no producers or executives telling us what to do. We were the creators."**
> Eric Idle

being swapped between teams. It was here that conflict could arise, particularly between the less laid-back Jones and Cleese, but in the early days such arguments were rare. There was only really one rule: was it funny? And that was something they invariably agreed upon.

In this show, everyone was to be both a writer and a performer, and the casting was decided in a similar democratic and equitable manner. They had all been performing since their university days and were up for taking on roles written by the others as well as themselves. Even Gilliam was roped in when required, or when there was some heavy make-up or an uncomfortable costume to wear.

By June, Ian MacNaughton had been confirmed as the director for Series One (although he would miss the first four studio recordings, with John Howard Davies standing in). MacNaughton had directed the *Q5* series, and the group believed his free-spirited and slightly anarchic directing style complimented their own vision. So, on Tuesday July 8, 1969, the first day of shooting for this most modern of comedy series took place amid the staid surroundings of London's 16th-century Ham House.

CIRCUS RINGMASTER

There was still the small matter of the name of the series to be decided. For a while, the group had loosely decided on *Bunn, Wackett, Buzzard, Stubble and Boot* (a football forward line-up from a Cleese sketch), while the BBC's memos continued to refer to *Barry Took's Circus*. A number of alternatives were suggested and rejected before they realized the 'Flying Circus' element was the part that would keep all parties happy. But whose Flying Circus was it to be?

Once again, a number of suggestions were mulled over, especially Michael Palin's suggestion of 'Gwen Dibley' (a name he had spotted in a Women's Institute magazine). Eric Idle came up with 'Monty' after a larger-than-life figure from his local pub and John Cleese

added the 'Python' to convey a slimy theatrical-agent-type character. Somehow it stuck – the BBC was happy to call it *Flying Circus* and the Pythons were pleased with their wry moniker.

In contrast, the title music and opening credits were decided upon without fuss. A meeting between MacNaughton, Palin, Jones and Gilliam focused on brass-band music and, from the selection at hand, Sousa's march 'The Liberty Bell' was selected. Gilliam could imagine exactly how it would work with his animation, while Palin wrote in his diary that he liked it for its upbeat feeling without being "calculated, satirical or 'fashionable'".

Gilliam's opening titles are described in the script for the first episode as "Titles beginning with words 'Monty Python's Flying Circus'. Various bizarre things happen." What follows is a taste of the animations to follow; a surreal chain of cut-out and montaged illustrations, Victorian and Edwardian photos and classical paintings, including the foot that finally ushers in the show's title, which is a transposed detail from the bottom right-hand corner of 'An Allegory with Venus and Cupid' by 16th-century artist, Bronzino.

PROPOSED SERIES NAMES

It's

You Can't Call a Show Cornflakes

Bunn Wackett Buzzard Stubble and Boot

Whither Canada?

Owl! It's Colin Plint

A Horse, a Spoon and Bucket

The Toad Elevating Moment

The Algy Banging Hour

Owl Stretching Time

Gwen Dibley's Flying Circus

Socks and Violence

Wodge Wodge Boodle Oodle Poo

The Venus de Milo Panic Show

Title Characters

It's Man

The story goes that the It's Man – as he would be known – was a once smooth-talking TV presenter given to loquacious introductions. Now fallen on hard times, he is bedraggled – dressed in rag and wild-eyed – but is determined to perform his televisual function… He announces nearly all of the first three series without ever getting past the word "It's".

Python convention dictated that the writer of a sketch or creator of an idea would usually be given the main role. At the outset of the first series, Michael Palin suggested a desperate, unkempt, castaway-type character should stagger out of ridiculously harsh surroundings and with his last breath attempt – and ultimately fail – to introduce the programme. The others embraced the idea and agreed that Palin would be perfect for the role. He had cause to regret the suggestion…

The brief films in the first series put Palin in a series of uncomfortable situations including,

being submerged in the sea, hung on a meat hook in an abattoir and crawling across a pebble beach. He even appeared in the end credits of episode three being mauled by a lion. In episode eight, there was a twist: his luck had appeared to change as we see him being attended by a bikini-clad woman passing him a glass of wine. A brief smile appears on the face of the ragged-dressed wild man before he realizes he has now been passed a bomb.

In the second episode of the third series, the It's Man (who had a vox pop in Series Two, saying,

"I would tax Racquel Welch. I've a feeling she'd tax me") stepped into his own sketch. A show, seemingly called *It's*, set in a swanky studio chat-show set reveals Lulu and Ringo Starr, pretty big stars of the time, sitting on the sofas. A voiceover prompts the entry of the show's host and, as the It's Man in his customary tattered clothes, emerges onto set, Lulu admires his look. Typically though, things are about to take a turn for the worse…

The signature tune and opening animated titles start. The It's Man, still visible through the

titles, tries in vain to stop them. The guests walk off in disgust. The It's man tries to drag them back. Failing, he sits down as the music ends. Fade out.

Continuity Announcer

The BBC had generally ceased to use in-vision continuity announcers by the mid-1960s. Previously though, in the post-war TV years, they had been a staple of the evening viewing schedule. Monty Python would make frequent use of such an announcer – typically sitting at a formal desk and usually dressed in a dinner jacket (as even BBC radio announcers were once required to wear).

In episode two of the first series, Eric appeared as the announcer, saying, "And now for something different. A man with three buttocks." It was the first time this phrase – which would become synonymous with the series and provide the title for the movie of re-shot sketches from the show – was uttered (although Aimee MacDonald had used it in *At Last the 1948 Show*). Michael gets to use the phrase later in the same show, but henceforth it would belong to John Cleese.

It would become a catchphrase in the second series, when it was also co-opted as part of the opening credits. John plays the staid BBC announcer in his dinner jacket completely straight, whether his desk is situated the middle of a field, in a zoo cage and even on a window cleaner's lift. By Series Three, the phrase had been cut to 'And now…' but viewers were well-versed enough by then to fill in the rest.

Nude Organist

T he final part of the triumvirate of figures in Series Three's openings is Terry Jones's Nude Organist. Initially played by Terry G as a tacky showbiz-style musician in the "Blackmail" sketch in Series Two, Jones took over the role for the third series. He created this bizarre figure with wild bouffant hair and wearing just a collar and tie, who would play his chord and turn to camera with a (sometimes blackened-tooth) grin. As with his fellow opening-title characters, as the series progressed, the Nude Organist would find himself in a series of far-fetched locations.

Nude Man: [Terry Jones] Well, I see my role in it as, er, how can I put it best – the nude man – as sort of symbolizing the two separate strands of existence, the essential nudity of man...
"The Man at the Organ", Series Three, episode 9

In episode 9 of the series, The Nude Organist nearly got an opportunity to explain himself. Sitting in a scarlet dressing-gown that has the name "Noël Coward" crossed out and "Nude Organist" written underneath, the organist is surrounded by a documentary film crew, make-up and photographers. He is full flow to a journalist, when the cue for his chords arrive and he pauses, hurriedly disrobes and continues his customary role.

"I only got the Nude Organist role because we decided to shoot him on location and Terry G never came on the filming trips." Terry Jones

SERIES ONE

In 1969, British TV comedy audiences could justifiably claim they had never had it so good. Classic series such as *Dad's Army* and *The Morecambe and Wise Show* were already up and running, and popular new series included Frankie Howerd's *Up Pompeii*, Carla Lane's *The Liver Birds* and *Doctor in the House* (co-written by Graham Chapman). The viewing public clearly had an appetite for laughs, but *Monty Python's Flying Circus* was about to present something completely different …

Filming for the series had taken place over the summer and, after a week's rehearsals at the Acton Working Men's Club, the team readied themselves for the first day of studio recording. On Saturday, August 30, in Studio 6 of BBC's Television Centre, Monty Python stepped out in front of a live crowd for the first time ever.

Although the 320-strong studio audience had applied for tickets, they were completely unaware of the type of show they were about to witness. No doubt many were expecting a real circus and the Pythons often compare that first audience to the stony-faced members of the Women's Institute who feature in the stock footage used in the series. In fact, Michael Palin recalls John Cleese saying before the show, "Do you realize this could be the first comedy show to go out with absolutely no laughs at all?"

Buoyed by some enthusiastic friends and family, the audience gave it a chance and some of the sketches earned some hearty laughs. So, at the end of the show, the slightly deflated Pythons felt they had something they could build on. It would be over a month before the series began broadcasting, so without press reviews and audience figures, they were still unsure how the show would fare.

The BBC had taken an incredibly laissez-faire attitude to the content of that first series, giving the Pythons artistic control that programme-makers today can only dream of. However, the corporation's scheduling was not so flexible. The group, and their rapidly growing band of followers, were frustrated that the series was initially broadcast late on Sunday evenings, generally between 10.45 p.m. and 11.15 p.m.

This late-night programming was often taken by religious or arts discussion programmes, and implied that the show was aimed at intellectuals – certainly not the youth and pre-teen audience it would eventually captivate. Moreover, the slot was subject to a regional opt-in – BBC areas

Above: The Pythons were very pleased with the chair allocation from the BBC.

such as the Midlands or the North East could, and would, choose not to show the series.

After the fourth episode, there was also a two-week break, when the show was replaced by a couple of arts documentaries. Co-incidentally, this was around the point when the series began to capture the public imagination. Studio recordings were now attracting a younger audience more sympathetic to the material and glowing press reviews had convinced the BBC management that the Pythons had a future. While audience figures for the early shows were around two million, this had doubled by the ninth episode, which went out in the more satisfactory prime-time slot of 9.45p.m.

On November 27, 1969, Michael Mills, the BBC's Head of Comedy, wrote congratulating John Cleese on the success of the series and offering a second series: "The shows seem to be getting better and better and this is a view shared by most people who see it," said Mills.

The evening after the final show, the whole team were interviewed by Joan Bakewell on BBC2's *Late Night Line-Up*. Not so long before, Palin and Jones had been contributing sketches to that same show. Now they were fêted guests – the *Flying Circus* was airbound.

"**Voiceover:** [John] When this series returns it will be put out on Monday mornings as a test card and will be described by the *Radio Times* as a history of Irish Agriculture." Series One, Show 12

Nearly half-a-century has passed since *Monty Python's Flying Circus* first hit the UK's small – mostly still black-and-white – television screens. With hindsight, this first series can be seen as Python attempting not perhaps a revolution in comedy as such, but certainly testing its limits. *Marriage Guidance Counsellor*, *Stolen Newsreader*, *Seduced Milkman* or *Secret Service Dentists* were very well written and executed, but were traditional fare. Elsewhere, however, in sketches such as *Whizzo Chocolate*, *Johann Gambolputty… of Ulm*, *Blancmanges Triumphing at Wimbledon* and *Albatross*, the silliness went off the scale.

"We use only the finest baby frogs, dew picked and flown from Iraq, cleansed in finest quality spring water, lightly killed, and then sealed in a succulent Swiss quintuple smooth treble cream milk chocolate envelope and lovingly frosted with glucose." Whizzo Chocolate, Series One, episode 6

The series succeeded in creating its own unique structure through the links. As well as Terry G's animations, the Colonel, Redcoat, the Announcer, the vox pops and the visual links were all funny in their own right. Most impressive of all was the wealth and diversity of ideas. The series was constantly inventive – for every parody of a BBC arts or debate show or a courtroom scene, there was something totally new, like *Wresting to Determine the Existence of God*, the Red Indian theatre-goer or the Vercotti brothers trying to run a protection racket on the army.

"We were unsure of what kind of reaction we were getting until around shows five and six. And then we started to get the feeling that there was an audience there for us." – Terry Jones

UPPER CLASS TWIT OF THE YEAR

This, one of the most famous of sketches, is a perfect example of how Python took the satire of the previous years and twisted it deliciously – ridiculing rather than savaging its subject. The term Sloane Ranger was still to be coined when the script was written but there was no doubt to the target of the sketch.

John Cleese was inspired by the behaviour of the Nigels and Tarquins who frequented a wine bar near his apartment in Kensington (although he later admitted to the *Philadelphia Inquirer*, "I met my first twit in prep school.") In particular, he took exception to them keeping him awake as they slammed the doors of their expensive cars – one of the key events in the contest along with Insulting the Waiter, Taking the Bras off the Debutantes and Shooting Themselves.

THE MOUSE PROBLEM

"Who here can say that they have never been sexually attracted to a mouse?" A supposedly hard-hitting documentary series, *The World Around Us* (which shares a theme tune with BBC's *Panorama*) investigates the growing social problem of men wanting to be mice. These deviants go to mice parties, where they eat cheese, squeak and dress up as mice. Written by the openly gay Chapman, the sketch is a classic satire on the controversy and outcry surrounding the emerging gay lifestyle of the 1960s.

It refers to the supposedly anonymous Mr A – whose real name and address are immediately provided. In the original recording, the phone number given was, in fact, David Frost's. Just two days after broadcast, the original stand-in director, John Howard Davies, sent a memo to Ian McNaughton, requesting that the caption voiceover be re-recorded, apparently to ensure that the BBC wouldn't "castrate" Davies again when the show was repeated.

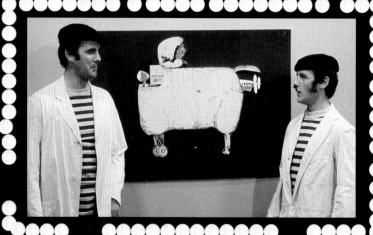

FLYING SHEEP

"A sheep is not a creature of the air; it has enormous difficulty in the comparatively simple act of perching..."

Cleese and Chapman had offered their sketch about sheep attempting to fly to *The Frost Report* a few years earlier, but producer Jimmy Gilbert had rejected it for being too silly. The two-hander, a discussion between a city gent (it's not really clear what he's doing there) and a surprisingly verbose, smock-wearing country bumpkin was exactly the kind of material that they had in mind for Python.

The sketch is followed by a companion piece in which Cleese and Palin speak in mock-French and leap around as they discuss their proposed ovine aviation venture. These sketches were the first to be recorded in front of a live audience – an important litmus test for the new show.

The French sketch had to be re-run after a moustache malfunction (it is a rare surviving out-take). However, the reaction of the audience to the second (and broadcast) version was noted. Both Palin and Cleese felt lifted by the laughter generated on a second take so early in the recording and their confidence in the show rose accordingly.

CANDID PHOTOGRAPHY (AKA NUDGE NUDGE)

Perhaps Eric Idle's most famous contribution to the Flying Circus appeared in the third episode of the first series. The sketch was preceded by a short link in which John Cleese interviews schoolboys Palin, Jones and Idle in the playground. The interview ends with the boys saying they want to see Nudge Nudge, a sketch young Eric has written.

In fact, Eric Idle had written the sketch for Ronnie Barker to perform on the *Frost on Sunday* show. It had been rejected, with Eric admitting that on paper the sketch did seem to lack jokes, but when he subsequently read it out at a *Flying Circus* script meeting, the reaction was totally different and the Pythons fell about laughing.

The sketch would become a favourite in the live shows. Its familiarity was greatly helped by Eric's adaptation and performance for an advert for Breakaway chocolate bar. In future live shows, Eric would pull out a bar during the sketch, before throwing it aside and exclaiming, "Urgh! Breakaway!" In Australia, Eric (and subsequently John as his brother) also recorded an advert for a car bumper called a 'Nudge Bar'. Eric has revealed that Elvis Presley was a huge Python fan and this was his favourite sketch. Elvis's then girlfriend, Linda Thompson, said the he would recite the sketch and would even address people as "Squire" in its honour.

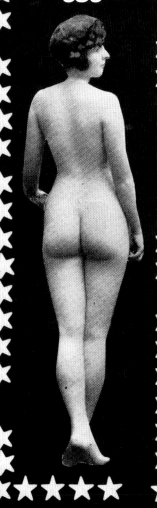
Bicycle Repairman

"Superman 1: Oh look... is it a stockbroker?
Superman 2: Is it a quantity surveyor?
Superman 3: Is it a church warden?
Supermen 1–3: NO! It's Bicycle Repairman!"
Recorded on the first day of filming, this was one of the first Python sketches to be completed. It features a world full of Supermen in which a mild-mannered bicycle mechanic (Michael Palin) lives incognito, only revealing his true identity – and overalls – when a cyclist needs his assistance. The brilliantly underplayed Jones–Palin sketch is augmented by a concluding commentary referring to the superhero's fight against World Communism. The commentator (John Cleese), broadcasting from a table in a pleasant garden, breaks into a hysterical, violently anti-commie tirade until he is told by his wife that his tea is ready.

Confuse-a-Cat

"Your cat is suffering from what we vets haven't found a word for."
Graham claimed the idea for this sketch originated when he and John Cleese were distracted from a writing session by a discussion on the immobility of a neighbour's cat. They decided the cat was suffering from complacency and was too comfortable in its frame of mind. The sketch begins with a couple's concern for their cat's well-being. Graham (always at his best playing medical men) is a vet who spouts nonsense with great authority, leading to a call to a well-drilled theatrical company who specialise in puzzling pets.

The Pythons performed the sketch on 1969's *Christmas Night with the Stars* (the sketch they submitted about a pet shop that modifies terriers into other animals was rejected). This showcased the BBC's best light-entertainment performers, including the *Dad's Army* cast, Cilla Black, Kenneth Williams and Dick Emery – *Monty Python's Flying Circus* had made it!

"I dare say some of the younger viewers have never seen it before because it does go out very late at night. Luckily, it is the one show I'm allowed to stay up for." Val Doonican introducing Monty Python performing Confuse-a-Cat on *Christmas Night with the Stars*, 1969

MR. HILTER AND THE NORTH MINEHEAD BY-ELECTION

The Pythons rarely wrote outside their teams or solo designations, but this sketch was an exception. According to Michael Palin's diary, John called him on the morning of Sunday August 3, 1969, inviting him over to Knightsbridge for an afternoon's writing. He records how, after initial awkwardness, they settled into writing a sketch about Hitler, Goring, Von Ribbentrop and Himmler living in a seaside guesthouse.

The Nazis, who are in (not very good) hiding, busy themselves at breakfast by plotting the invasion of Stalingrad – although "Mr Johnson" helpfully points out that they have the wrong map and need the Ilfracombe and Barnstaple section, and planning their local election campaign. The sketch is original and great fun and leaves one wondering what else the Palin–Cleese writing team could have come up with if they weren't established with their writing partners.

Hell's Grannies

The antics of the hoodlum widows of Bolton (shot in East Acton) are the focus of yet another iconic early Python sketch. Although initially a traditional reversal-of-the-norm sketch, with grannies attacking teenagers, the Pythons make it memorable with meticulous humour and fine acting, from Eric Idle's over-earnest sociologist-presenter and John Cleese's terrorised yobbo to Graham Chapman's concerned grandson. The sketch is then Pythonised by the appearance of baby snatchers and vicious gangs of 'keep left' signs, before concluding with the Colonel's last-ever *Flying Circus* appearance.

The Restaurant Sketch

As a couple order their meal at a well-heeled restaurant, a casual reference to a dirty fork is the catalyst for a snivelling apology, extreme self-flagellation and a little violence. Sometimes referred to as the "Dirty Fork" sketch, it also features John as a very Basil Fawlty-like Mungo the Chef. The sketch also gave the group a chance to mock the traditional punchline by announcing it with a title card and getting the audience to jeer at its delivery.

WHIZZO BUTTER

"Watch for clever animated sketches by artist Terry Gilliam. He takes Old Masters and brings them to life." So wrote the *Sunday Post* in its preview. Apart from the opening titles Gilliam, who had a separate credit as animator until episode six, would take centre stage early in the first episode. It was a taste of things to come, with a head being cracked open like an egg and renaissance angels surrounding a pack of butter. George Melly, writing in the *Observer*, was an early fan, praising Gilliam's work, and explaining, "They owe something technically to Max Ernst's collages, rather more to 'Yellow Submarine', but the way they are used is totally original."

THE FUNNIEST JOKE IN THE WORLD

Over the years, the Pythons have had to explain many times that the so-called killer joke – "*Wenn ist das Nunstruck git und Slotermeyer? Ja! ... Beiherhund das Oder die Flipperwaldt gersput!*" – is in fact, pure gibberish; just some German words, some German-sounding words and a sentence structure that appears to be German. The sketch was an ambitious ten-minute assembly of parodies of news footage, documentaries, archive clips and war films, and, in the discovered edited sections in the archive, even includes a wartime memory and part of a speech from Winston Churchill.

THE LUMBERJACK SONG

I'm a lumberjack and I'm okay
I sleep all night, I work all day

He's a lumberjack and he's okay
He sleeps all night and he works all day

I cut down trees, I eat my lunch
I go to the lavatory
On Wednesdays I go shopping
And have buttered scones for tea

He cut down trees, he eat his lunch
He go to the lavatory
On Wednesdays he goes shopping
And has buttered scones for tea

He's a lumberjack and he's okay
He sleeps all night and he works all day

I cut down trees, I skip and jump
I like to press wild flowers
I put on women's clothing
And hang around in bars

He cuts down trees, he skips and jumps
He likes to press wild flowers
He puts on women's clothing
And hangs around in bars

He's a lumberjack and he's okay
He sleeps all night and he works all day

I cut down trees, I wear high heels
Suspendies and a bra
I wish I'd been a girlie
Just like my dear mama

He cuts down trees, he wears high heels
Suspenders and a bra...

This simple song about the day-to-day life of a cross-dressing tree-feller appears on every list of popular Python sketches. Originating as a typical Python exit to the "Homicidal Barber" sketch, where the reluctant hairdresser expresses his frustrated ambition to be a Canadian lumberjack, it has evolved into a highlight of the live show.

Michael Palin clearly recalls the sketch's conception. "It was the end of the day – around 6.45 – and Terry J and I were still stuck for a conclusion to the barber sketch," he remembers. "We suddenly came up with this ending where he gets up and says, 'I don't want to do this anyway. Fuck this, I want to be a lumberjack!' From there the words to the song came easily and we were finished in half an hour."

During rehearsals, the song was worked out with Fred Tomlinson, whose singers were regulars on the show, and on the night of the studio recording, Michael Palin, unused to singing in public, nervously stepped forward with his "best girl" Connie Booth (John Cleese's wife at the time). To the side stood the Mountie chorus, the Fred Tomlinson Singers, augmented by John Cleese and Graham Chapman, selected, according to Graham, because of their Mountie-like height.

Soon after its debut in episode nine, Michael sung a German translation ("The Holzfäller Song") in Monty Python's Fliegender Zirkus and it begun its journey to become one of the great British comic songs of all time. A highlight of live shows, it has been sung by both Michael and Eric, although across the years the Lumberjack's "Dear Mama" has become a "Dear Papa").

Among the song's many instant admirers was Python superfan, George Harrison. The former Beatle used it as a curtain-raiser on his 1974 American solo tour, produced the song when it was released as a single in 1975 (it reached number 51 in the charts and maybe would have done better if they had all agreed to perform it on BBC's Top of the Pops TV show) and appeared as a Mountie singer in the City Center live show in New York in 1976. In tribute, the song was performed at The Concert for George at the Royal Albert Hall in London in 2002 by Michael Palin with Carol Cleveland at his side and Terry Gilliam, Eric Idle, Terry Jones and Tom Hanks in the chorus.

SERIES TWO

Series One made an impact. The late-night audiences had averaged around three million and press reaction had been almost unanimous in its acclaim. The show had also garnered three BAFTA nominations (for Best Light Entertainment Show, Best Script, and John Cleese for Best Light Entertainment Personality) and received two special BAFTA awards (for production, writing and performance, and for Terry Gilliam's animations).

Alan O'Brien said in the *New York Times*, December 1969: "Childlike yet sophisticated, surrealist and simple-minded, it provides an outlet for the team's personal obsessions, group fantasies and nightmarish anecdotes … the connection linking their involved sketches, silent-film action sequences and animated graphics with the real world is oblique and tenuous. But the inside-out dream logic nevertheless exists."

Despite individual projects, the Pythons eagerly began writing another series. They had a confidence borne of the success of the first series and had learned how they could improve. They had new ideas and were prepared to re-work sketches that they had rejected for their debut season.

In March 1970, the BBC contracted Monty Python for another 13-episode season of *Flying Circus*, with filming to begin in May and studio recordings in June. Having held out for a bigger budget, they were able to film sketches as far afield as Norwich, Kent, Walton-on-Thames and Devon – even a visit to Torquay, which brought them face-to-face with a strangely rude hotelier, who subsequently inspired John Cleese to create Basil Fawlty.

Despite the positive response to the first series, the BBC announced that the new season would go out at 10.10 p.m. on Tuesdays, beginning in September 1970, preceded by repeats of five episodes from Series One in the same slot. Yet again, it was a time when regions could opt out and screen items of local interest instead, so 26 episodes would be broadcast with almost half the country unable to view them.

The Pythons were appalled, as was the national press, as typified by Sean Day Lewis's attack in the *Daily Telegraph*: "Five regions again opted out of *Monty Python's Flying Circus*, quite the most ludicrous calculation of programme planning the corporation has managed for many a year."

Tickets for the new show were now taken up by the growing army of Python fans. Michael

Palin describes how, in the first recording for the series (episode 12) "… even in our completely straight red-herring opening – the start of a corny pirate film which went on for nearly five minutes – there was a good deal of laughter, just in anticipation."

The show was broadcast from September to December 1970 and included a two-week break after episode four. The first of these was to allow *The Horse of the Year Show* to be broadcast. The show-jumping event was a 1970s TV-audience favourite, but even though it only replaced *Flying Circus* on one occasion, it has become a mythical example of how Python was treated so

Above: The full cast (plus extras) of Series Two of *Monty Python's Flying Circus*, demonstrating how not to be seen.

disdainfully. Even in 2014, Michael Palin told the *Daily Telegraph*, "Every now and then they would take us off and run *The Horse of the Year Show* instead."

Many consider Series Two to be the highpoint of the *Flying Circus*. The style and structure of the show was familiar to fans, but the stream-of-consciousness style flows effortlessly, the sketch ideas have taken a step into the ridiculous, they are unafraid to play visual jokes and the animations are bolder in nudity, violence and sheer imagination.

The main change to the new season was in the opening of the programme. Now there was a much shorter It's Man sequence followed by a dinner-jacketed John sitting at a desk to

proclaim the phrase now fully associated with the show: "And now for something completely different." Moreover, the conventional opening, including music and credits, was increasingly a moveable feast, sometimes not appearing until well into the show.

"I'd like to answer this if I may in two ways. Firstly, in my normal voice and then in a kind of silly high-pitched whine …"

The series features the now-customary TV parodies, from *Face the Press* to the gameshow *Blackmail*, some great filmed gags such as *The Semaphore Version of 'Wuthering Heights'*, *How Not to Be Seen* and *The Exploding Version of 'The Blue Danube'*, rather a lot of *The Man Who...* (*The Man Who is Alternately Rude and Polite*, *The Man Who Contradicts People*) and more brilliant left-field flights of fancy, including Raymond Luxury-Yacht requesting plastic surgery, killer sheep and the Test Match that finds a spin dryer bowling to a table.

"No, no. It's spelt Raymond Luxury-Yacht but it's pronounced Throat-Wobbler Mangrove!"

The final show went out on Tuesday December 22. It would next appear on the agenda at the following day's BBC Controllers' meeting.

With the last show of the series, Python had at last managed to shock the BBC management into noticing them. It had been less than respectful to the Queen, featured heavily bandaged patients being forced to work, a sketch about cannibalism in the Navy complemented by gruesome Gilliam animation, and, finally, the gross-out bad taste of "The Undertakers". At Wednesday's meeting, some on the board deemed it "disgusting", while Head of Programming, Bill Cotton, said, "The team seemed to have some sort of death wish." The Pythons' card had been marked.

The Ministry

John Cleese's bowler-hatted minister takes an extraordinary Whitehall walk – a finely choreographed and marvellously straight-faced performance of over-extended and twisted limbs – into comedy legend. Indisputably one of the UK's favourite TV sketches of any era, it has an app of its own, an annual Silly Walk March in Brno, in the Czech Republic, and a silly-walking bowler-hatted figure even features as the sign for a pedestrian crossing in Ørje, Norway.

The idea emanated from a Cleese/Chapman session, during which they saw a strangely stooped man negotiating the steep hill outside. However, they passed the idea onto Palin and Jones, who developed the sketch. They created an imaginary ministry, where silly walks vie with Defence, Health and Social Security, and where a hopeful Mr Pudey petitions for a grant to develop his own silly walk. He is unsuccessful, but does manage to gain a place on the Concorde-type, Anglo-French project 'La Marche Futile'.

Although the dialogue itself is top-class, Pythonesque "satire", it is Cleese's

PIRANHA BROTHERS

In March 1969, the Kray Twins, Ronnie and Reggie, were found guilty of murder at the Old Bailey and sentenced to a minimum of 30 years in prison. The trial had been big news and the notorious East End gangsters were household names and ripe for parody – especially now they were safely behind bars.

Hard-hitting documentary series Ethel the Frog's telling of the story of the notorious Piranha Brothers, Doug and Dinsdale, mirrors the Krays' history. Without fear of repercussions, the sketch mocks their childhood, the police corruption that surrounded them, the real-life DS 'Nipper' Read and even alludes to Ronnie's homosexuality, although the torture methods more closely resemble those of their rivals, the Richardsons, who had been sent down in 1967. Even the Spiny Norman character has been said to be a nod to Sergeant Norman Pilcher, who gained notoriety for his pop-star drug busts.

# of Silly Walks

famous walk that accounts for the sketch's popularity, but there is one person who claims never to have enjoyed it – John Cleese. He has said, "The only reason it became so iconic was the brilliance of my performance, because I never thought it was a very good sketch." Failing to remove the sketch from the live shows, he would bait Michael Palin mid-set with his hatred of it and was relieved in later years to excuse himself from performing it at all on account of his artificial knee and hip.

"On the first night that we did it in the show in Brighton, the first time we ever did it onstage, I did it to complete silence; it was appallingly embarrassing. I was doing all this stuff and the audience was just sitting there. It was awful, and I said, 'You see?' I came off, I was triumphant, I said, 'You see, it's no bloody good. I never want to do it again.' And they said 'Oh, please, please do it just once more tomorrow.' And I went on the next night and the bastard audience laughed. And then I was stuck with it. I was stuck with the bloody thing and I had to do it every night." *John Cleese*

Bruces

On the face of it this is one of the most dated *Flying Circus* sketches, based, as it was, on long-outmoded and crude stereotypes. And yet "Bruces" has remained a live favourite and consistently ranks high in fan polls – even in Australia.

The philosophy professors at the made-up University of Woolamaloo, all of them named Bruce, welcome a new member, Michael Baldwin, whom they decide to call "Bruce" to avoid misunderstanding. The sketch is a cascade of 1970s Aussie clichés, from khaki outfits with matching cork slouch hats and right-wing attitudes to forthright banter and anti-intellectualism (the Bruce who teaches logical positivism is also in charge of the sheep dip).

The sketch was created by the unusual combination of Eric and John. It was influenced by the media coverage of the Queen's visit to Australia in early 1970, Barry Humphries' boorish "Barry Mackenzie" comic strip and, according to Eric, his Australian friends in London, including film producer, Bruce Beresford (later to direct *Driving Miss Daisy*).

Eric remembers the starting point for the sketch was the idea that Australian philosophers as a concept was, in itself, amusing, while John recalls, "It seemed like an odd thing. It was just a funny idea – lots of philosophers all called Bruce."

the EXPLODING VERSION of THE BLUE DANUBE

Spanish Inquisition

Credit for one of Python's most repeated phrases is laid firmly at the feet of Michael Palin. "When Mike first read The Spanish Inquisition out to me, I was gobsmacked – how on earth had he got to that?" Terry Jones recalls, while Michael himself says that it just came naturally. He was writing the 'trouble at the mill' section and as soon as he hit upon the 'no one expects' line it fell into place.

The appearance of the three cardinals (Palin as Ximénez, Jones as Biggles and Gilliam in a rare and a memorable acting role as Fang) at the utterance of the throwaway phrase was heightened by Ximénez's difficulty counting and the comfort of their instruments of torture. The rack turns out to be an ordinary washing-up rack and, in the following scene, they produce soft cushions and a comfy chair.

Their appearance is further noteworthy for the final word of the episode. Having arrived at the Old Bailey just too late to utter his introductory phrase, Ximénez utters the expletive, 'Bugger!' In 1970, this was still a risqué word, even on late-night television, and its use was questioned by BBC management. Surprisingly, BBC Head of Comedy, Michael Mills, allowed it to stay in, having watched the recording and agreed it was a fitting expletive.

Cardinal Ximénez also appears in episode four, *The Buzz Aldrin Show*, where he displays problems counting the number of aftershaves he uses. However, later in the episode, when the chemist in the Police Constable Pan Am sketch provides the 'didn't expect' cue, PC Pan Am just tells him to shut up.

GRAHAM CHAPMAN

b. January 8, 1941 (Capricorn)

GRAHAM ~~is~~ was a polymath. Able to turn his hand to almost anything. Capable of doing *The Times* crossword in less than a second, he ~~is~~ was quite sure that he could have found Higgs-Boson up in his attic if anyone had asked. He's was a qualified doctor, trained at the famous Jack the Ripper Hospital in London's East End, where his specialty was the throat, and what to put down it. His skill in the kitchen ~~is~~ was legendary. Brought up on Lemon Curry, Graham enjoyed experimenting with new and unusual combinations. There ~~is~~ was no such thing as a light supper at the Chapman household and dazzled guests ~~are~~ were likely to be served anything from Duck on a Chair, Pork and Savlon Terrine to his signature dish - Lip of Peccary, wrapped in warm pages of *Pilgrim's Progress* and garnished with the very top of Giant Redwood Trees.

Graham ~~is~~ was drawn to the unorthodox like a fish to water. A founder member of the Dangerous Sports Club, he ~~likes~~d nothing more than to run up a huge bill – sorry, hill – and come down it on a piano. The hill, not the bill. Graham ~~has~~ had a fearsomely low boredom threshold. He ~~admits~~ admitted to going to sleep in *King Lear*, even though he was playing him at the time. In the evening before bed he'll often write an opera. Criticised by some as derivative, few can doubt the power of *Ron Giovanni, The Tring Cycle* – a 12-hour drama set in the Job Centre of a small Hertfordshire town – and *La Triviata*, the story of a woman obsessed with board games. And if he ~~has~~d any spare time, Graham ~~likes~~d nothing more than to go out onto the terrace of his Palladian semi in Harlow and, literally, wrestle with his conscience.

JOHN CLEESE

b. October 27, 1939 (Scorpio)

JOHN CLEESE comes from a long line of criminal deviants in the Bristol area. For almost 60 years, the Cleese Family ran the Avon and Somerset children's party circuit with legendary ruthlessness. Their protection methods were feared across the region. At one time it was estimated that for every balloon sold in Greater Bristol, 3p went to the "family". Clowns disappeared mysteriously from the Clifton Suspension Bridge and the fire brigade were regularly called to rescue children from Sid the Sword-Swallower (later discovered to have been one of the Cleeses).

John was very different. A shy, introverted boy with a love of authority, he was the first of the Cleeses to get into Cambridge without using a tunnel. He found early on that he had a talent for making people laugh. He just had to stand there, really. Though John could have been many things – a lawyer, a cordwainer, or even a flautist – he decided that being laughed at was for him. With a group of marginally shorter people (some, like Bill Oddie, much shorter), he put together a show called Cambridge Circus, which took New Zealand by storm.

From then his career took a dive. *The Frost Report*, *At Last The 1948 Show*, *Fawlty Towers*, *Life of Brian* and *A Fish Called Wanda*, were all seen as cries for help. In later years he spent increasing amounts of time with the dysfunctional Monty Python team, many of whom are here tonight.

John is the Founder and CEO of Wives For Men, an organization which campaigns to stop people being married to the same woman for too long. Of his friend and fellow Python Michael Palin, he once said, "See what I mean."

TERRY GILLIAM

b. November 22, 1940 (Sagittarius)

UNFORTUNATELY for Terry Gilliam his beginnings were fraught with difficulty. Due to a dodgy sense of direction he failed to complete the journey down his mother's birth canal and was never officially born.

It was only after a couple years of discomfort for both the unborn and parent that his mother realised something was amiss down under and set off for Australia, not to solve the immigration crisis racking the island, but for an illegal backstreet operation involving a chainsaw, a didgeridoo and two fork-lift trucks. The young Gilliam was successfully removed from what was left of his mother and, for the doctor's safety, wrapped in newspaper and dumped in the pouch of a kangaroo doing life in a nearby prison, where he grew to manhood.

In the course of his life he has been played by a variety of actors, layabouts, conmen and stilt walkers.

Incredibly, for a man who wasn't born and has been unable to keep a job for more than a few days, he has made a name for himself. Sadly, in the 1960s, that name was Richard Nixon.

As the Vietnam War heated up he was forced to make a difficult decision: leave the country or become President of the United States of America. He chose the high road, changed his name and set out for England.

Always a romantic, like so many of his generation, he rejected the pampered, powdered, salons of Mayfair and chose to live the hard life, marching arm in arm with the common man. He found employment in the Yorkshire coal mines, working alongside his childhood hero, Arthur Scargill. But his dream was short-lived once again, thanks to the unfortunate name he had chosen during his escape from America: Margaret Thatcher.

Having twice chosen badly, he was determined that this time he would assume a name that would be so vapid and meaningless that all of his ambitions would never again be stymied: Tony Blair.

As we know, history proved him right. Not only did he go on to become Prime Minister of Britain, free Kosovo, rid the world of two monstrous and deceitful dictators, bring peace and understanding to Iraq, and more recently, happiness to the entire Middle East, but also, miraculously, he achieved all of this without the loss of a single life of anyone important.

Although now working full time for Rupert Murdoch, during the Python reunion, Terry will be appearing under his own name.

ERIC IDLE

b. March 29, 1943 (Aries)

ERIC IDLE was born in March 1943 in a railway siding near Doncaster, a month earlier near Newcastle and then finally three weeks later in Tesco's in Oldham.

He was sent down the mine at the age of four and became only one of fourteen armed miners to stage a revue which shut down the entire North East Coalfield, but which earned high praise from the *Sunday Times* and encouraged him to go to Russia, where he wrote a novel about D. H. Lawrence called *Lawrence of A Labia*.

Dropping out of school he joined the army at eight, before being asked to leave for upsetting the other boys.

It was near Sutton Coldfield that he would first discover the man who would later become Michael Palin, hiding in a wood, making a documentary about people who hide in a wood near Sutton Coldfield. It was to be the start of a lifelong journey for both of them, across the very heart of Sutton Coldfield, which gave rise to a very long personal joke, the Sutton Coldfield joke, which no one has ever been able to understand …

'Hey, Mike, what about Sutton Coldfield then?'
'Nor 'alf.'

He has appeared at the end of the Pier and at the end of a Peer, though the charges were later dropped, and even worked for a while as a waitress in a Joan Collins novel. Summer stock in Bridlington led to him being discovered by Val Parnell for *Night of The Big Noses*. He played Guinevere in *Othello* at the National Theatre (a surprise to many of the other actors) and has since been nominated for three Gertys, a DAFTA, a Britcoin Award, as well as twice winning *Wanking With the Stars*.

Eric thanks God for giving him all his big chances, and the Police for not noticing.

He is thrilled to be working alongside Sarah Palin.

TERRY JONES

b. February 1, 1942 (Aquarius)

TERRY JONES was born in a two-up two-down maisonette in Paris, where he lived happily all his life. Only occasionally venturing out into the wide world, where he encountered dragons and demons and all sorts of vengeful creatures that would tear your eyes out as soon as look at you. He later in life got accustomed to these dragons and demons and became best friends with them, occasionally playing Snap (a card game) and Snakes & Ladders (a bored game).

On the December 6, 1945 (age three), he was introduced to enormous fish that could probably have swallowed him whole, but he fought his way out of the fish and then succumbed to the Black Death. Sometime later he was introduced to another even more enormous fish but he managed to escape and then again succumbed to the Black Death. No one knows how he survived the Black Death, but there are stories of him consorting with the Devil and other saints.

Terry Jones first came across the other Pythons in Calcutta where they were cleaning out the sewage system. He suggested to them that they should get together and form a comedy team/troupe/group, but they weren't really interested, they were engrossed in the intricacies of the Calcutta sewage system, whether one tunnel led to another or simply stopped, or whether a tunnel could lead to another tunnel and yet another tunnel and, if so, what did this signify? Terry told them not to waste their time on the Calcutta sewage system, but they were adamant. They said he was infringing their personal freedom to do what they wanted, and would he please go away. So he went away and that is why Monty Python's Flying Circus has never existed.

MICHAEL PALIN

b. May 5, 1943 (Taurus)

Born in Sheffield in 1943, Michael Palin was immediately regarded by everyone who knew him as a brilliant bloke. He got lots of good marks at school and was a cracking good centre-half at football. He was great at university and terrific in all the things he did afterwards. There's nothing this top geezer can't turn his hand to. He even writes his own biographies.

As the editor of the Official Python Biographies I must apologise for the inadequacy of the previous biography. Michael unfortunately suffers from ACLOAWGOAHAAPTS (A Complete Lack Of Attention to Whatever's Going On Around Him At Any Particular Time) Syndrome. This makes it impossible for him to concentrate on anything for more than 11 seconds. He's on the list for a brain transplant but they haven't been able to find one that fits. In the meantime I have been asked to provide a more comprehensive guide to those who want to know more about the life of a typical ACLOAWGOAHAAPT sufferer.

Michael was born close to scaffolding during the dark days of World War Two. His inimitable humour was clear right away when his first scream was an uncanny take-off of the scream of Lord Beaverbrook, then Minister of Supply in the wartime coalition.

His mother did her best, but even she found it impossible to keep a straight face as he did his "Ooh where's my buttock now Mrs Percival?" routine as she struggled to change his nappy. Immediately after the war the then Minister for Labour, George Isaacs, on visiting Michael's home town of Sheffield, heard his now legendary sheep joke – "How many sheep does it take to change a light bulb? Ooh never you mind!" – and fast-tracked Michael through his education so that he could entertain the nation in the dark times of post-War austerity. He was just six and a half when he became the youngest ever Derek Dingle Scholar at Oxford's prestigious Balliol College. After three hilarious years reducing some of the greatest minds of his time to quivering jellies, he caught the eye of Tom Williams, then Minister of Agriculture, who brought him to London to study humour under Maxwell Silverhammer, Britain's Funniest Jew.

With sharp Yiddish repartee now allied to his talent for extreme physical comedy – he once ran all the way from London to the Balkans just to slip on a banana skin outside Zagreb – he was ready for the ultimate accolade – the chance to work with the Fab Five – John "Get Your Own Grapefruit" Cleese, Eric "Who's that Under My Bed" Idle, Terry " There Goes Another Acorn" Jones, Terry "Four Smiles" Gilliam and the unforgettable Graham "Light My Trousers" Chapman. The rest is history: Edward IV 1461–83, Edward V 1483, Richard III 1483–85, Henry VII 1485–1509, Henry VIII 1509–47, Edward VI 1547–53.

(That's enough history – Ed)

from the archives...

.(AT THE DOOR IS A PEPPERPOT IN
SAME CARPET SLIPPERS AND PAISLEY
DRESSES AS THE OTHERS WORE,
EXCEPT SHE HAS OVER IT A
MILKMAN'S OVERALL, HAT,
MONEY BAG AND APRON)

4TH PEPPERPOT:
Milko!

(AND ONE SMASHES MILK BOTTLES
OVER HER HEAD.

JEREMY THORPE, OUTSIDE THE
DOOR, LEANS INTO SHOT. AND GRINS
AND WAVES BRIEFLY. SHE SLAMS THE DOOR)

JEREMY THORPE SHOULD BE ABSOLUTELY
ACCURATE, MAYBE A MASK NEEDS TO
BE MADE.   HE HAS HEAVY FIVE
O'CLOCK SHADOW, TRADITIONAL
THORPE TRILBY, ETC. AND A LARGE
YELLOW ROSETTE.)

INTO PYTHON TITLES.

AFTER TITLES.   COME TO A ROLLER
CAPTION SUPERED OVER A STILL
OF A DRAWING OF A WESTERN
CAVALRY FORT.   (SEE TERRY G.)
WESTERN STIRRING MUSIC OVER.

V.O.:
In the spring of 1863 the

Comanches rallied under their

warrior leader Conchito, in a final,

desperate attempt to drive the white

man from the rich hunting lands of

their ancestors... The U.S. Cavalry

were drawn up at Fort Worth and the

scene was set for a final all-out

onslaught that could set the new
territories ablaze.

ACTION   SOUND

SCENE 1.   FILM. (OPENING)

MAN:
It's

JC.VO. —

M P'sFC .

SCENE 2: ANIMATION

Titles beginning with words
BUNN WACKETT BUZZARD STUBBLE
AND BOOT. Various bizarre
things happen. When the
titles end.

STUDIO:

SCENE 3: ANNOUNCER'S DESK

(ORDINARY GREY SUITED ANNOUNCER
STANDING BY DESK. HE SMILES
CONFIDENTLY)

ANNOUNCER:
Good evening.

(THE ANNOUNCER CONFIDENTLY
MOVES TO CHAIR AND SITS DOWN.
THERE IS A SQUEAL AS OF A BIG
BEING SAT UPON)

- 1 -

SCENE 32. FILM: 10 See Music
M.P. pushes pig down

(2)

(357)

ₜ2
~~8~~ min 33 SeeS

1 min 43 into an.
    ~~235~~ Sec ~~Saturday~~

of all the fun at the fair,
    Ervin's Merenyi

(SPLIT SCREEN OR MONTAGE OF
ARTISTIC ACTIVITIES, EDITED
LIKE SPORTSVIEW AND WITH SPORTSVIEW
MUSIC OVER.   (A PAINTER, A SCULPTOR,
A COMPOSER AT PIANO AND TENNYSON
ON THE MOORS, A CONCERT..ALL STOCK
FILM)   Saturday Sports
            Wilfred Burns

(AFTER A FEW SECONDS OF THIS
A VOICE OVER SAYS)

J.C

V.O.:
Hold it!

Woman is pushing man sitting on
chair, pushes him off, everytime she
says sit up she hits him, Another
lady comes in and says the same.
the man's body is pulled up, and
squashed down, CUT.

V.O Sit up, S,U, S.U,

V.O Sit up

V.O help me out.

Woman sitting on chair with very
full skirt on someone is under it, a little girl comes on screen
makeing noises, her head disappears
and the noise is louder, a man's head apears
where the womans was, general speaks
rubbish, hand comes out of mouth

SCENE 33.

CUT TO GILLIAM ANIMATION FILM.

see notes

(USUAL RUBBISH ENDING WITH
PIG SITTING ON MAN. THERE IS
SHOUT OF PAIN FOLLOWED BY
'Get Off'.

Victorian
Confusion

CUT TO STUDIO:

MONTY PYTHON'S FLYING CIRCUS WITH VERY F~~EW NAUGHTY WORDS~~

Last Episode

~~XXXXXXX~~ EPISODE 13

'At last, a real work of art' Don Revie

'I laughed till I dried' I.McKellen.

'Much better than a poke in the eye' Connie Francis.

for. 2 p.m. 4.30 - 11.30

Tue. 10 a.m. 2-6 dub.

30th ~ 1st. editor.

MONTY PYTHON'S FLYING CIRCUS : SERIES THREE SHOW 13

Cast list as on screen:

Conceived written and censored by

Michael (Bulky) Palin

Terry Jones (King of the Lash)

John Cleese (A smile a song and a refill)

Terry Gilliam (An American in plaster)

Graham (A dozen wholesale) Chapman

Eric Idle (Actual size, batteries extra)

Also appearing

Carol Cleveland (Four revealing poses. Hard publication price 40P)
In a variety of interesting positions, the Fred Tomlinson
Singers under their leader 'Butch' Tomlinson
Roasalind 'Afore you go' Bailey Now available from BBC Enterprises
for 30P and a bottle of Bells

Body Make up

Madelaine Gaffney and the BBC Naughty ladies club

Unusual costumes and leatherwear

Hazel Pethig and the Naughty lads of 'Q' Division.

Rostrum Camera mounted by

Peter Willis (Massage in your own home or hotel room)

Animations and erotic cartoons

Terry Gilliam and Miss Hebbern 043- 7962

Graphic details

Bob Blagden (Denmark has never laughed so much)

Red Lighting

Bill Bailey

Heavy breathing and sound

Richard Chubb

V/O   Oh come on you can give us another minute
      Mr Cotton, please.

CAPTION   Conjuring today

CONJURER   Good Evening, last week we learned how to
           saw a lady in half This week we going
           to learn how to saw her into 3 bits + dispose
           Of the body ... aaark!

   POLICE CHASE CONJURER ACROSS STAGE.

MAN   look if you can put on rubbish like that + horse of
      the Year Show, you can afford us another minute
      Mr Cotton please I mean look at this load of ---

   FADE TO BLACKOUT

      Add * here ---

MAN: (CONTD.)
So near is it to Oros that the
Ape Monsters of Oros are able to
leap onto the Earth as it spins
helplessly and Mr. Neutron,
in a last bid for survival enlists
the help of the Black Forces of
Mordor who, in league with the hideous
Saturnians, hurl the Apes of Oros,
into the galaxy of Ginead and
the fires of eternity.   That's
how it ends really.

(CLEARS THROAT)

- Spins off into Space
there are appallingly
expensive scenes of
devastation + horror +
the final incredibly
expensive climax is read
as thousands of Ape
Monsters in very expensive
costumes descend from
the sky, plus up a whole
city which had to be specially
built + fling them all into
the sea very expensively.
And we can see those very
expensive scenes right now

LOOKS AT TV AS CREDITS
ROLL ~~AS CRE~~

AFTER A MOMENT OR TWO HE GETS UP
AND LEAVES THE STUDIO.

CUT TO EXTERIOR TV CENTRE AS HE
COMES OUT.   HUGE HAMMER HITS HIM.

~~ROLL CREDITS.   NEIL'S SONG.~~

~~PROTEST SONG.   OVER STOCK FILM OF~~
~~HUGE AREA DEVASTATED BY WAR~~
~~(HIROSHIMA)~~

MAN
Just after the credits. Incidentally
these are going to be some of
the most lavish + expensive
scenes ever filmed by the
BBC in conjunction with
Time-Life ... those are some
of the technical people who
have been involved in
filming these expensive scenes
expensive sound, expensive
visual effects there,
expensive designer, cheap
director And you can see
those expensive scenes
right now

VO:
World Domination tea-shirts are
available from the BBC, World
Domination Department, Room 13,
Near Cardiff.

BLACKOUT

Add right at the
end.

CAPTION
The End

-72-

MENU

EGG + SPAM	1.50
BACON + SPAM	1.60
SAUSAGE + SPAM	1.99
EGG BACON + SPAM	4.10
BACON SAUSAGE + SPAM	4.50
SPAM SAUSAGE SPAM EGG + SPAM	6.70
SPAM SPAM SPAM SPAM SPAM SPAM + EGG	8.90
SPAM SPAM SPAM EGG BAKED BEANS + SPAM	9.99

Although, thanks to Monty Python, 'spam' is now more frequently used as a catch-all term for unwanted emails, it was originally a tinned, preserved and processed meat that kept the masses fed during the hard times of World War Two. By the more affluent late 1960s, spam was synonymous with cheap, unappetising, tinned food – and it sounded funny.

The sketch features the fictional Green Midget Café in Bromley, South-East London, where spam accompanies every dish on the menu and a group of Viking customers (the Fred Tomlinson Singers – again) lead a rousing chorus of The Spam Song – a ditty containing few words apart from "spam". There follows a re-appearance of the Hungarian from the Phrasebook sketch and a historian who explains the great Viking voyage from Trondheim to Bromley. The words of both are eventually liberally peppered with the word "spam", as are the final credits.

The sketch was penned by Palin and Jones. Terry J recalls it being received well by the others, but John and Graham offered to work on it to improve it. "They made it much more logical and rational, but lost all the tempo and rhythm, and that was what Mike and I saw as making it funny." When it came to the recording, the original sketch was re-instated.

PRA:(CONTD.)
Hatters, Hat Block and Ian Makers,
Hatcheries, Handbag Frame
Manufacturers, Heraldic Artistaes,
Hide Skin Fat and Wool Manufacturers,
Hinge Improvers, Hoopers, Hose
Clippers and Couplers, Hygiene
Services, Handrail and Balustrade
Companies, Horn Carvers, Hoist Welders,
Hub Cap polishers, Handreaders,
Hoteliers of all waters, Horticultural
Sundriemen, Hop Growers, Hearing Aid
Suppliers, Hair and Bristle
Specialists, Honey Merchants, Hobby
Shops, Herbalists Hengineers,
Hypnotherapists, Mr. Heron of
Hounslow, four times, Hi-Fi Knowalls,
Heating Contractors, Hardcore
Depositories, Handkerchief
Repairers, Highland Outfitters,
Harbour Authorities, Handle Makers,
The Hippopotamus Boutique a Go-Go,
Hacksaw Salesmen, Hincome Tax
Consultants, Hutters, Hirers of
Hydrogen Helium and Hoxygen to Her
Highness, Ha le Selassie Huncle Don,
and a Ham Crere from Epping, a
veritable mish-mash of tradesmen
jostling for me favours.

SOUND
ACTION

RICHARD III.
A horse!! A horse!! My Kingdom
for a horse!! (TERRIFIC
GESTURES ETC).

SPECIALIST.
Most of these cases are pretty
unpleasant, but the treatment
does work on some people. This
chap for instance came to us
straight from the Chichester
Festival, we operated just in
time, and he's now almost normal.

(HE CALLS OVER A VERY ORDINARY
RICHARD III, WHO SMILES
DISARMINGLY AND SAYS QUITE
CHATTILY)

2ND RICHARD III.
A horse, a horse my kingdom for
a horse.

SPECIALIST.
But in here (MOVING OVER TO DOOR)
We have some very nasty cases
indeed...

(HE OPENS DOOR, FROM HERE
GILLIAMS FEVERED, NOT TO SAY
FEVERISH, IMAGINATION LEADS US
INTO THE WACKI WORLD OF
...WARD WINNING GRAPHIC HUMOUR,
WHERE COMEDY IS KING IN A NO
HOLDS BARRED JOKE J.MBOREE
THAT'LL HAVE YOU THROWING
YOURSELF INTO THE FILMES.)

(BUT EVEN THIS JOLLY JOKESMITH
FROM ORIENTAL COLLEGE MUST
CONTROL HIMSELF AND PROVIDE
US WITH A LINK INTO 'FLOWER
ARRANGEMENT'.

DELICATE MUSIC. STUDIO SET.
FLOWERS IN VASES ETC. SUPER
CAPTION 'FLOWER ARRANGEMENT'
THEN ANOTHER CAPTION 'INTRODUCED
BY D.P. GUMBY'.)

GUMBY.
Good evening, first take a
bunch of flowers. (HE GRABS
FLOWERS FROM VARIOUS VASES
AROUND HIM) Pretty begonias,
tulips, irises, freesias,
then arrange them in a vase.

(HE THRUSTS THE FLOWERS HEAD
DOWNWARDS INTO THE VASE AND
STUFFS THEM IN WILDLY, HE EVEN
TREADS ON THEM TO GET THEM ALL
IN)

GUMBY.
Get in! Get in!

(MIX TO FILM. A TYPICAL SHOT OF
WILD FLOWERS IN BEAUTIFUL ENGLISH
COUNTRYSIDE. GENTLE PASTORAL
MUSIC. THE CAMERA BEGINS TO PAN
AWAY FROM THE FLOWERS, MOVING
SLOWLY ACROSS THIS IDYLLIC
SCENE. MIX IN THE SOUND OF
LOVERS - THE INDISTINCT DEEP
VOICE, FOLLOWED BY A PLAYFUL
GIGGLE FROM THE GIRL, AT FIRST
VERY DISTANT, BUT AS WE CONTINUE
TO PAN IT INCREASES IN VOLUME,
UNTIL WE COME TO REST ON THE
SOURCE OF THE NOISE - A TAPE
RECORDER IN FRONT OF A BUSH.

　　　　　　　　/CONTD....

"FISH LICENCE"

"Why should I be tarred with the epithet 'loony' merely because I have a pet halibut? I've heard tell that Sir Gerald Nabarro has a pet prawn called Simon. You wouldn't call Sir Gerald a loony would you!"

The return of John Cleese's Eric Praline, our hero from the "Parrot" sketch, produces a less-well-known sketch, but one that is beloved by many Python fans. Still wearing his plastic raincoat, occasionally speaking direct to camera and inclined to the odd loquacious phrase, this is a slightly more eccentric Praline, who attempts to buy a 'fish licence' for his pet halibut named Eric (it transpires he also has a dog, cat and fruit bat all named Eric, for which he has licences). In live shows, the sketch would conclude with John's favourite song, "Eric the Half a Bee". The sketch is interrupted by Praline had already appeared in episode five of this series, where he starts to present a half-hour chat show with his flatmate, Brooky (Eric Idle). The sketch is interrupted by Terry J as a floor manager, explaining the scene has been cut. Ironically, the recorded sketch was cut, but the original script was discovered in the Python archives.

Right: An excerpt from the unused and never broadcast script of the Praline Chat Show.

Intern

Monty Python's Fliegender Zirkus

IN 1971, BETWEEN SERIES TWO AND SERIES THREE OF THE FLYING CIRCUS, WHILE THE BBC WERE STILL DEBATING WHETHER MONTY PYTHON WERE WORTHY OF A NATIONAL TV SLOT, THE BAVARIAN CHANNEL WDR DECIDED THIS MOST ENGLISH OF COMEDIES WAS CERTAINLY WORTHY OF A GERMAN AUDIENCE.

"They came to us, saying, 'Look, we haven't got a sense of humour, but we understand you do. Can we use yours?'" Eric Idle

The idea was the brainchild of legendary German talk-show producer, Alfred Biolek, who had taken a liking to *Flying Circus* on a visit to England. After failing to persuade the group to join forces with German-speaking comedians, Biolek hatched a new plan for the Pythons to write two special shows for the German market.

"It was a strange offer which, of course, made it seem more interesting and attractive to us." John C leese

The shows were to use only filmed material, but the sketches were largely original. The group came up with a mixture of German-orientated sketches, pieces with an Olympic theme (West Germany would be hosting the 1972 Olympics a few months after the show was broadcast) and the usual Python TV satire and nonsense.

Though they wrote the scripts in English, it was to be translated and performed in German. Only John appeared to have any acquaintance with the language, so this would clearly present a difficulty. "I still claim to this day," says Michael, "that I only found out we were performing the sketches in German once we arrived in Bavaria!" The sketches would be learned parrot-fashion, usually on the evening before filming.

"There was a marvellous feeling of mutual bafflement and bewilderment from both us and the German crew." Michael Palin

The episode featured a typically wacky piece on German painter Albert Durer, a surreal version of *Little Red Riding Hood* (starring John as a brilliantly butch, un-dainty heroine), *The Merchant of Venice*, performed by the Cows of the Bad Tolz Dairy Herd, and a sketch set in a "traditional" Bavarian restaurant, where the waiters indulge in strange Bavarian traditions. It is, however, probably best remembered for "The Lumberjack Song" – sung by Michael in phonetically learned German – and "The Silly Olympics", an excellent re-versioning of the "Upper Class Twit of the Year" sketch.

"Announcer (John): Hello, sport lovers. We're here on this beautiful morning at the 27th Silly Olympiad. First, at the high point of the day, the 100 metres for men with no sense of direction. Olasen, the Silly Swedish Gold Medallist, is in the rear lane. [The starter shoots his gun, and they all race in different directions. Cut to another field.] And now the next final, the 5000 metres for the deaf. [The starter shoots his gun, and the runners all stay there. Cut to a swimming pool.] Now the 2,000 metres breaststroke for non-swimmers. [The swimmers jump into the pool and don't get out.] We'll be bringing you back here when they fish out the corpses. Now over to the sign of the marathon for incontinent people."
"The Silly Olympics"

The show was broadcast on January 3, 1972 to a slightly confused but generally welcoming public, although the language issue loomed large. Audiences struggled to understand much of the Pythons' hurriedly learned German, and the speed and emphasis with which the lines were delivered ruined much of the comic timing. Nevertheless, it was successful enough for WDR to commission another episode. This time it was performed in English and dubbed into German, with Biolek, perhaps diplomatically, explaining that it would help international sales.

In September 1972, the Pythons returned to Bavaria to record the second episode. This show re-used Graham Chapman's "One Man Wrestling" sketch from his university revue and "The Hearing Aid" sketch from At Last the 1948 Show, but had a new fairy tale

written by John and Connie Booth, and a couple of gems in the Klondike-style Panning for Chickens and the ever-popular "Philosophers' Football Match". The latter set a team of Greek philosophers against a line-up of German thinkers plus the real-life Franz Beckenbauer, Germany's greatest-ever footballer – "Obviously a bit of a surprise there."

"I remember filming the "Philosophy Football" where Cleesey [Archimedes] crossed from the right and I [Socrates] scored a great diving header." Eric Idle

"The Germans are disputing it. Hegel is arguing that the reality is merely an a priori adjunct of non naturalistic ethics, Kant, via the categorical imperative, is holding that ontologically it exists only in the imagination, and Marx is claiming it was offside."

The show was transmitted in the evening of December 18, 1972. It was once again well received by the limited audience it reached, but alas the station executives were unwilling to continue the project. Still, it was fun while it lasted.

"During the shooting, word came that the station's management were unhappy with the uncut material they had seen – they called us 'dilettantes', which rather pleased me!" John Cleese

THE PEPPERPOTS

"There is a particular type of middle-aged woman who uses irritation as a way of life. It's the only thing she's really good at. She's roughly this shape – like a pepperpot … A Pepperpot's life's ambition is to be in the audience at a quiz show. She is to be found in shopping areas, blocking the pavement, tormenting babies, spreading rumours and spending a fortune on bargains. She enjoys worrying and being shocked. Individually, she is intolerable. In a group, horrific." John Cleese, *How to Irritate People*, 1969

The Pepperpots – a moniker generally credited to Graham Chapman – might have pre-dated Python, but there are few *Flying Circus* episodes where the shrill-voiced, manly women didn't make their mark. Today, the group admit that the female roles they wrote lacked a certain depth. Although the exceptions are memorable – John as the prissy Anne Elk or Eric glammed up as Veronica Smalls – Python women tended to be either glamorous, often scantily dressed girls played by actresses (usually Carol Cleveland) or sexless, middle-aged harridans – the Pepperpots.

"… I mean they're not even married or anything, they're not even divorced, and he's in the KGB, if you ask me. He says he's a tree surgeon, but I don't like the sound of his liver, all that squeaking and banging every night till the small hours …"
"The Court Scene", Series One, episode 2

In his book, *Monty Python VS The World*, Jim Yoakum tells how a visit to a tea shop by Graham Chapman and his partner, David Sherlock, inspired early Pepperpot traits. David describes how these "mad creatures" – the elderly lady shop owners – were mistrustful of their new electric till, checking the addition by hand. By the end of the *Flying Circus*, however, the Pepperpots had shown a penchant for classic art galleries, an in-depth knowledge of modern French philosophy and a propensity for extreme violence.

Although easy to dismiss as a homogenous stereotype, each of the Pythons played their Pepperpot characters slightly differently. Graham's would be loud and brash, Eric's often had a gleam in their eyes and a slight sense of naughtiness, Michael's were usually dear old ladies and John's verged on the bizarre. Terry J., however, was the master (mistress?) of versatility,

with a range that went from shrewish to homely. Pepperpots could be characters in sketches, in links (often vox pops), but also shared some great sketches themselves.

WHIZZO BUTTER
An interviewer asks a group of Pepperpots if they can tell the difference between Whizzo Butter and a dead crab. They can't, but one of them (Terry J.) menacingly adds that if the interviewer who usually asks women that were to ask them the same question, they'd slit his throat.

ART GALLERY
In between giving a good slap to the unseen infants accompanying them, Marge (Graham) and Janet

★★★ ★★★★★
PEPPERPOT NAMES

MRS PREMISE
MRS CONCLUSION
MRS NESBITT
MRS SMOKER
MRS NON-SMOKER
MRS THING
MRS ENTITY
MRS CUTOUT
MRS CONCRETE
MRS GORILLA
MRS NON-GORILLA
MRS MOCK TUDOR
MRS ELIZABETH III
MRS SCAB

★★★★ ★★ ★★★

(John) discuss their toddler-trawling art-gallery experiences. Little Kevin has besmirched Raphael's Baby Jesus with Ketchup and tucked into 19th-century British landscape artists, while young Ralph is a spitter and was able to splat one on a Van Gogh from some distance.

EXPLODING PENGUIN ON THE TV SET
Another John-and-Graham classic finds two Pepperpots discussing the penguin that has appeared on top of the television. Theories to its origin range from next door, to the Antarctic, to the zoo. John recalls that it took around 14 takes for them to get it right due to their constant corpsing, especially when Graham shouts "Burma!" for no logical reason.

"Pepperpot 1 [Graham]: How does Dr Bronowski know which zoo it came from? Pepperpot 2 [John]: He knows everything. Pepperpot 1: Oooh, I wouldn't like that, that'd take all the mystery out of life. Anyway, if it came from the zoo, it'd have 'Property of the zoo' stamped on it." Series Two, episode 9

MRS PREMISE AND MRS CONCLUSION VISIT JEAN-PAUL SARTRE
A Pepperpot discussion about putting down budgerigars leads to Mrs Premise (John) and Mrs Conclusion (Graham) travelling to Paris, where they meet Jean-Paul Sartre and discuss his classic text *The Roads to Freedom*.

"Mrs Premise [John]: He didn't join in the fun much. Just sat there, thinking. Still, Mr Rotter caught him a few times with the whoopee cushion. Le capitalisme et la bourgeoisie, ils sont la meme chose … Oooh we did laugh …" Series Three, episode 1

1969 Series One live recording ticket. BBC recording events were free and open to the public, who could apply for tickets to attend.

MONTY PYTHON'S FLYING CIRCUS

White City Station (Central)

T.V. Centre, Wood Lane
T.V. Theatre, Shepherds Bush Green
T.V. Studios, Lime Grove

Wood Lane

Shepherds Bush Station (Metropolitan)

Uxbridge Road

Shepherds Bush Station (Central)

M.41

Holland Park Ave.

Lime Grove

Shepherds Bush Green

Goldhawk Road

Shepherds Bush Rd.

Holland Road

Goldhawk Road Station (Metropolitan)

BUS ROUTES

■ 72,105,295,220
● 12,207,49,72,105,220,295
◆ 12,88,117,105,220,49,207

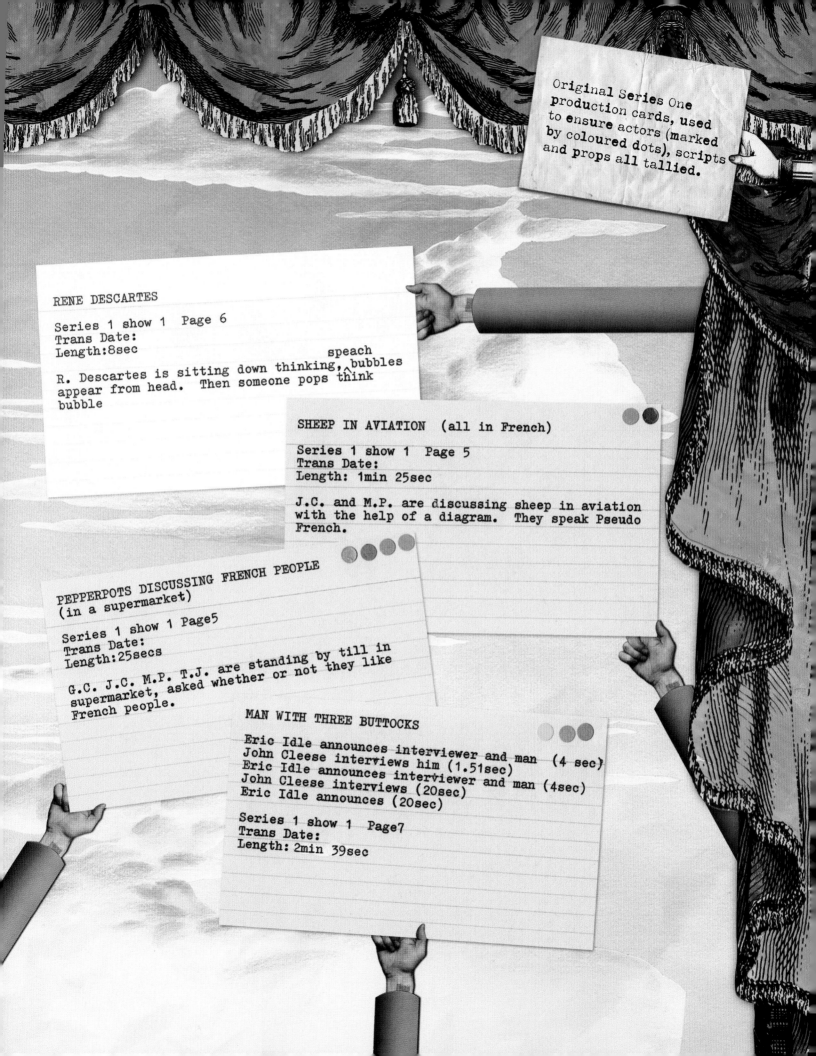

RENE DESCARTES

Series 1 show 1   Page 6
Trans Date:
Length:8sec

R. Descartes is sitting down thinking, bubbles appear from head. Then someone pops think bubble

SHEEP IN AVIATION   (all in French)

Series 1 show 1   Page 5
Trans Date:
Length: 1min 25sec

J.C. and M.P. are discussing sheep in aviation with the help of a diagram. They speak Pseudo French.

PEPPERPOTS DISCUSSING FRENCH PEOPLE
(in a supermarket)

Series 1 show 1 Page5
Trans Date:
Length:25secs

G.C. J.C. M.P. T.J. are standing by till in supermarket, asked whether or not they like French people.

MAN WITH THREE BUTTOCKS

Eric Idle announces interviewer and man   (4 sec)
John Cleese interviews him (1.51sec)
Eric Idle announces interviewer and man (4sec)
John Cleese interviews (20sec)
Eric Idle announces (20sec)

Series 1 show 1   Page7
Trans Date:
Length: 2min 39sec

SERIES THREE

By the time the second series ended, in December 1970, Monty Python had become a household name. Despite the following year's lack of new episodes, their profile remained high and a re-run of Series Two drew as many as ten million viewers each week (half the episodes were shown nationwide at 8.30 p.m.). A Montreux Comedy Festival Silver Rose award, a successful movie, *And Now For Something Completely Different*, featuring re-shot sketches from the TV series, a best-selling book and an audio record that reached number 26 in the UK album charts had all kept the Python flag aloft.

Despite such success, a further series of *Flying Circus* seemed in doubt for much of the year: John had some reluctance about continuing with the same format, Terry G had concerns about his fee, and all the group were involved in other projects. However, by August, they had eventually committed to recording a new 13-episode series for transmission in the autumn of 1972.

Shooting began in October 1971, with the filming as usual taking them across the UK, including sites in Glencoe, Scotland ("Njorl's Saga" – they would return here to film *Monty Python and the Holy Grail*), Bognor Zoo ("Life and Death Struggles"), Denham ("Literary Housing Developments"), Jersey ("The Cycling Tour"), Chislehurst ("The Third Test") and Windsor ("Elizabethan Porn"). The first seven studio recordings were made in the first two months of 1972, the remainder shot in April and May. Ominously, the group were surprised to see both Bill Cotton, BBC Head of Light Entertainment, and Duncan Wood, Head of Comedy, attending the final recording.

The challenge with the new shows was how to continue producing fresh and different comedy, in line with the original *Flying Circus* manifesto. As Michael said in an interview in the *Sun*, "Audiences become accustomed to anything in the end, even an anti-format show." The Pythons' response was to be even more controversial and include sketches and lines that seemed designed to shock. Unfortunately, a nervous BBC management, on high alert after "The Undertakers" sketch and other issues from Series Two, were now on their case. They demanded to see all the episodes prior to transmission, leading to the now infamous memo listing "32 points of worry" and a number of edits.

Like naughty schoolboys, the six Pythons were called in to explain a series of transgressions, ranging from the line "Your Majesty is like a dose of clap" from "Oscar Wilde" to a giant

penis (actually a severed leg) John was accused of waving in "Curry's Brains". Eventually, the BBC executives decided they were prepared to let these and some other misgivings go, but they stood their ground on other issues.

Duncan Wood's demand that the word masturbation had to be cut met with Terry G's famous defence: "Duncan, what's wrong with masturbating? I masturbate. You masturbate, don't you Duncan?" leading to a tense atmosphere in the office. The words "silly

Above: Series Three was made after the highly successful movie *And Now For Something Completely Different*.

bunt" were removed from the "Travel Agent" sketch (later to be reinstated in audio and live performances) and the "Wine-tasting/Wee-Wee" sketch was cut completely.

The series was transmitted between October 1972 and January 1973 at 10.15 p.m. on BBC1. Once again, audiences and the press loved it. In the *Sunday Times*, Peter Lennon described it as "... nothing short of inspired. Anarchy at its most exuberant and most richly comic." While Phillip Purser in the *Daily Telegraph* wrote, "Every kind of nudge and every brand of fantasy were triumphantly juggled together by sheer breathless energy."

The series would see the Pythons stick to their surreal mix of studio and film recording, and traditional and bizarre sketches, but the transitions and links between sketches appeared smoother and there were clear attempts to extend

the format. Just as they had added John's announcer to the It's Man opening, they now added the Naked Organ Player (Terry J having taken the role over from Terry G), playing fast and loose with the opening and closing of the programme, sometimes running the opening credits well into the show or having a fake ending with still minutes to run. As Michael noted in his diary, "We have finally thrown off the formal shackles of the *Frost Report* and we now miss very few chances to be illogical and confusing."

Although sometimes viewed as one of the weaker of the *Flying Circus* series, in fact the third season contained some of the Pythons' most diverse work to date. More experienced writing and acting produced as many treasured sketches as any of the other series, and some of Terry G's animations more than match his previous output.

The series included superb flights of fantasy – sketches such as "Whicker's Island" (a parody of British globe-trotting documentary presenter, Alan Whicker), the bloody "Sam Peckinpah's Salad Days" or the "British Naval Expedition to Lake Pahoe" – that came of confident writers working with a larger budget. It also had its share of classic Python silliness in "Gumby Brain Specialists", "Olympic Hide and Seek" and "The Queen's Own Kamikaze Highlanders", as well as forgotten gems such *as* "Gestures to Indicate Pauses in Televised Talk", "New Housing Developments" or the execution scene from "The Cycling Tour".

"We interrupt this programme again, A, to irritate you and, B, to provide work for one of our announcers."

Arguably, it is Eric Idle who emerges as the star of the series, with many of his contributions standing out. At the very start he delivers a stunning performance from the dock in the opening "Multiple Murder Court Case" and, in various guises, he brings to life "The Money Programme", "The Man Who Speaks in Anagrams", "Travel Agent" and "Party Hints by Veronica Smalls".

"Last week I showed you how to make a small plate of goulash go round 26 people, how to get the best out of your canapes, and how to unblock your loo. This week I'm going to tell you what to do if there is an armed communist uprising near your home when you're having a party."

"Party Hints by Veronica Smalls"

FISH—SLAPPING DANCE

This inane, absurd and perfectly executed 20-second sketch was performed for the *Euroshow 71* special. The "folk dance" is performed by Michael, wielding two small pilchards, and John, armed with a large halibut. Michael consistently cites it as his favourite Python sketch, saying, "We were so intent on getting the dance right that I didn't notice the lock had cleared and instead of it being a 2ft drop into the water it was a 15ft drop. Still, it was worth it, there's just something so fundamentally silly about it."

THE MONEY SONG

The advent of the Euro may have made the lyrics sound dated, but "The Money Song" remains one of the best *Flying Circus* musical numbers. Eric moves into it from his role as a serious financial programme presenter in an effortless progression – made absurd only by the appearance of the Fred Tomlinson Singers in traditional Welsh women's costumes. It was Eric's first venture into on-screen song, but he would go on to be the group's musical driving force, writing 'Always Look on the Bright Side of Life', 'Sit on my Face', 'The Galaxy Song' and many others.

"I've got ninety thousand pounds in my pyjamas,
I've got forty thousand French francs in my fridge,
I've got lots of lovely lira,
Now the deutschmark's getting dearer,
And my dollar bill could buy the Brooklyn Bridge."

ARGUMENT CLINIC

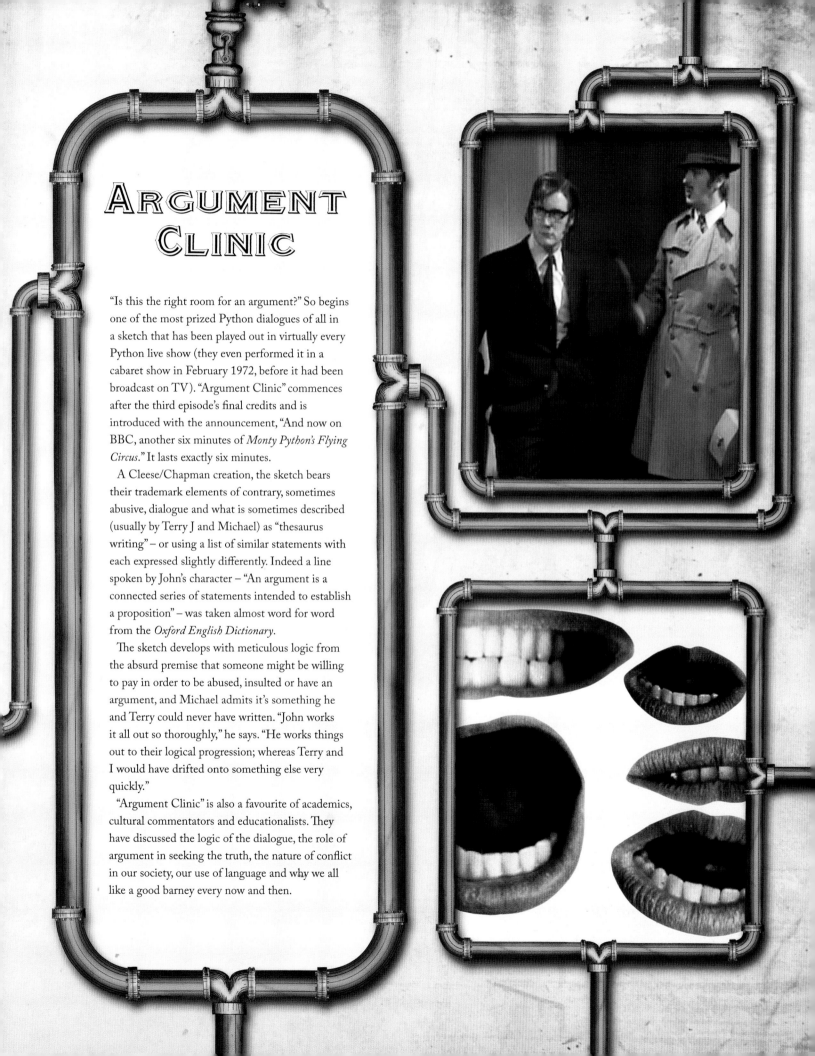

"Is this the right room for an argument?" So begins one of the most prized Python dialogues of all in a sketch that has been played out in virtually every Python live show (they even performed it in a cabaret show in February 1972, before it had been broadcast on TV). "Argument Clinic" commences after the third episode's final credits and is introduced with the announcement, "And now on BBC, another six minutes of *Monty Python's Flying Circus*." It lasts exactly six minutes.

A Cleese/Chapman creation, the sketch bears their trademark elements of contrary, sometimes abusive, dialogue and what is sometimes described (usually by Terry J and Michael) as "thesaurus writing" – or using a list of similar statements with each expressed slightly differently. Indeed a line spoken by John's character – "An argument is a connected series of statements intended to establish a proposition" – was taken almost word for word from the *Oxford English Dictionary*.

The sketch develops with meticulous logic from the absurd premise that someone might be willing to pay in order to be abused, insulted or have an argument, and Michael admits it's something he and Terry could never have written. "John works it all out so thoroughly," he says. "He works things out to their logical progression; whereas Terry and I would have drifted onto something else very quickly."

"Argument Clinic" is also a favourite of academics, cultural commentators and educationalists. They have discussed the logic of the dialogue, the role of argument in seeking the truth, the nature of conflict in our society, our use of language and why we all like a good barney every now and then.

THE MAN WHO WHO SPEAKS IN ANAGRAMS

There is a clue to the first sketch when the opening credits announce the start of "Tony M Nypot's Flying Riscuu", but after footage of explosions, fire and natural disaster and the start of a programme called *Blood, Devastation, Death, War and Horror*, it is surprising to find Eric introduced as a man who talks entirely in anagrams.

This is perhaps exactly the kind of sketch the group might have written for *The Two Ronnies*, but Eric completely owns the difficult, autocue-less performance. The end of the sketch is particularly priceless as he comes out of character when pulled-up for using a spoonerism instead of an anagram, saying, "If you're going to split hairs, I'm going to piss off."

The closing credits of the episode continue the fun with anagrams of all the names (except Carol's).

Cops and Robbers

As visually impressive as they are, not all Terry G's animations were concerned with violence and nudity. This perfectly crafted insert shows how he was able to create a full 30 seconds of entertainment from a single, simple joke. The robber's demand of, "OK buster, hands up!" being obeyed by the multi-handed victim is a funny, one-line cartoon gag, but around it there are images, sound effects and brief movements that deftly reflect the live-action humour.

NOVA II
SDMIDAB
M. NYPHOT'S
FLYING
RISCCU
SAW CODVENICE, TWITNER
DNA FORDEPERM YB
HAMRAG PACHMAN
JOHN ECLES
RICE LIED
MICHAEL LAPIN
MARTY RIGELLI
SOLA GAERAPPIN
CAROL CLEVELAND...

"New Housing Developments"

"Sam Peckinpah's Salad Days"

TRAVEL AGENT

Eric Idle's legendary tour-de-force as the irrepressible Mr Smoke-Too-Much, ably abetted by Michael's initially enthusiastic but soon worn-down Bounder of Adventure, became an unmissable element of Python live shows. After Carol Cleveland mistaking his visit for something more naughty, the joke about his name and the explanation of his inability to say the letter "C", Mr Smoke-Too-Much embarks on an inspired rant for three full minutes, hardly pausing to draw breath. The enduring popularity of the rant is incredible, especially as, more than most Python sketches, it is rooted in its early-1970s origins. Package tours, particularly those to the Spanish Costa del Sol, had become very popular in the late 60s and the monologue has many obsolete cultural references such as Instamatic cameras, Watney's Red Barrel beer, Entero-Viaform diarrhoea tablets and Timothy Whites pharmacies.

Unfortunately, much of the last section and the short "reprise" which concludes the broadcast episode are obscured by other action, dialogue and audience laughter, but they are captured in the original scripts.

"The Golden Age of Ballooning"

"Tudor Jobs"

"Marriage Counsellor"

FLY WITH US GETTING THERE IN COMFORT

ANNE ELK'S THEORY

John Cleese wasn't particularly happy in drag, but you wouldn't think it watching his cherished performance as Anne Elk. As Anne discusses her theory on brontosauruses, for which she is insistent on taking full credit, his prim delivery makes this sketch special. Her stuttering attempts to get to the point were apparently inspired by the speech mannerisms of Graham's partner, David Sherlock (who was also an inspiration for "The Man Who Speaks in a Very Roundabout Way").

The original script contains an introduction that never appeared on the *Flying Circus* broadcast, but was later used in an audio version of the sketch:

> "Presenter [Graham]: Good evening. Tonight dinosaurs. I have here sitting in the studio next to me an elk (he leaps out of his chair) Ugghh! Oh! I'm sorry. Anne Elk. Mrs Anne Elk."

With a jokey script note for the cast and crew:

> "The phone beside him rings. He answers it and while Anne Elk drones on as described below he intersperses her droning with the following: THIS IS WHAT THEY ARE WHICH HE SAYS."

There is also a rather hard-to-hear second Anne Elk theory stating that
"fire brigade choirs seldom sing songs about Marcel Proust."
The original script has an unbroadcast comment at the very end, where she admits – over the sound of fireman singing, "Proust in his first book wrote about..." – that:
"The second theory is obviously full of holes."

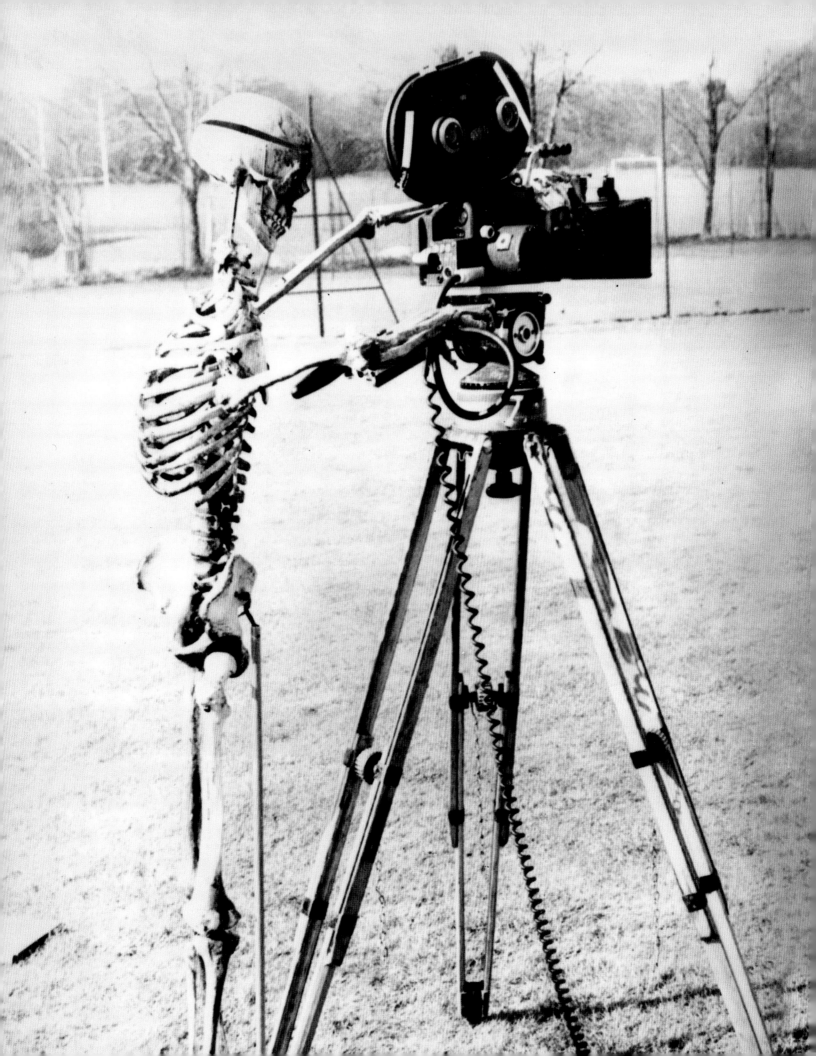

THE CHEESE
SHOP

In the TV series *Almost the Truth*, John Cleese recalls how the idea for the "Cheese Shop" sketch came about. He tells how he and Graham were in the car, returning from Folkestone, where he had been tremendously seasick while filming. Graham had advised him to eat something to settle his stomach, but the only thing he could face was a piece of cheese. They passed a chemist, which led them to discuss what kind of cheese a chemist might sell. The next day they decided that it was a good idea for a sketch, but why would someone be going to a chemist for cheese? Because the cheese shop didn't have any? Now there was an even better idea for a sketch…

John needed some persuading by Graham that the sketch was actually funny, but he had a great respect for his writing partner's opinions on humour. Even then it took Michael's reaction – he laughed hysterically until he fell off his chair – for him to realize they were really on to something. Michael, of course, played the straight-faced shopkeeper and both he and John have admitted that performing the sketch has been one of the most enjoyable aspects of the live shows, as they compete to force one another to corpse.

Red Leicester

Tilsit

Caerphilly

Bel Paese

Red Windsor

Stilton

Gruyère

Emmenthal

Norwegian Jarlsberger

Liptauer

Lancashire

White Stilton

Danish Blue

Double Gloucester

Cheshire

Dorset Blue Vinney

Brie

Roquefort

Pont-L'eveque

Port Salut

Savoyard

Saint-Paulin

Carre-de-l'est

Boursin

Bresse Blue

Perle de champagne

Camembert

Gouda

Edam

Caithness

Smoked Austrian

Sage Derby

Wensleydale

Gorgonzola

Parmesan

Mozzarella

Pippo Creme

Danish Fimboe

Czechoslovakian
Sheep's Milk Cheese

Venezuelan Beaver
Cheese

Cheddar

Ilchester

Limburger

THERAPY IN PROGRESS

TIME'S UP!

PIT STOP

LIVE NOW PAY LATER!

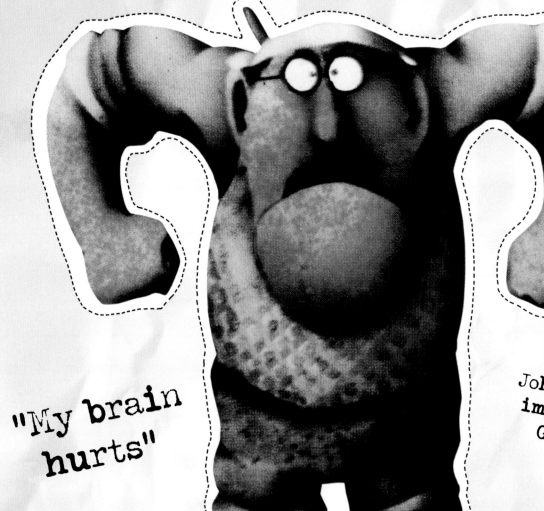

THE GUMBYS

The Neanderthal stance, eccentric dress and grunt-like speech of the Gumby is an enduring image from the *Flying Circus*. Series One, episode 5, saw the first documented appearance of a Gumby, in a sketch written by Michael. As played by John, a Gumby stood in a stream, calling for a tax on people who stand in water.

Although the script specified the gum boots (perhaps the origin of the name), Michael gives credit to Cleese and costume designer, Hazel Pethig, for the visual appearance of the Gumbys, who are something of a cross between a stereotype of a 1950s British working-class man at leisure and a village idiot.

"FIRST TAKE A BUNCH OF FLOWERS ... PRETTY BEGONIAS, IRISES, FREESIAS AND CRYMANTHESUMS ... THEN ARRANGE THEM NICELY IN A VASE."

"GUMBY FLOWER ARRANGING", SERIES TWO, EPISODE 12

By the studio recording of episode 9, they were established enough to be mentioned in the costume list: "5 Mr Gumbies: Wellies, long trousers rolled up to the knee, braces, collarless shirts, V-necked sleeveless pullovers (Fairisle), all too small for the wearers, white knotted hankies on heads." Although most beloved of Michael Palin, all the Pythons would eventually take a Gumby role (Terry G contributed an illustrated version, but didn't get to wear the cherished hankie until the final 02 show).

While there was no plan to incorporate the Gumbys as recurring characters, the Pythons obviously liked them and found increasing opportunities to include them in links and sketches. The best-loved of these include "Gumby Crooning", "Gumby Flower Arranging" and "Gumby Brain Surgery", from which the often-repeated "My brain hurts!" cry originates.

Their love of banging bricks together (often with their heads in between) and their monosyllabic words of "wisdom" made them ideal vehicles for parodies of academics and authority figures. They remained interchangeable and identified by their two initials, such as flower arranger D.P. Gumby – except John's Professor of Architecture, Enid Gumby.

The Gumbys would become a Python trope and an eagerly anticipated part of both the studio and the live shows. Roars of laughter would greet their arrival and they would often find rows of audience members sitting in wellies, tank tops and knotted handkerchiefs.

TIME LIFE
TELEVISION

Time & Life Building / New York, N.Y. 10020

PROMOTION KIT

MONTY PYTHON - 4

The BBC's official Series Four promotion kit. These were circulated to the press and other "interested parties".

MONTY PYTHON

COMEDY   Six half hour programmes

Illustration by Terry Gilliam

TIME-LIFE TELEVISION

Series Four

(Over)

MP4-3 MICHAEL PALIN AS QUEEN VICTORIA AND BOB RAYMOND AS HER ATTENDANT.

A BBC-TV Production

MONTY PYTHON 4

IN COLOR

TIME LIFE TELEVISION   TIME LIFE TELEVISION

MP4-1 (L. TO R.) TERRY JONES, MICHAEL PALIN, TERRY GILLIAM, ERIC IDLE AND GRAHAM CHAPMAN.

A BBC-TV Production

ONTY PYTHON 4

IN COLOR

MP4-2 TERRY JONES AS JOSEPH MONTGOLFIER ASSISTS CAROL CLEVELAND AS ANTOINETTE.

A BBC-TV Production

TIME LIFE TELEVISION

MONTY PYTHON 4

IN COLOR

TIME LIFE TELEVISION

SERIES FOUR

"Asked if the BBC were falling over themselves for a new series, a Python spokesman said, 'Nobody has fallen over. In fact there has been a great lack in falling.'" *Melody Maker*, December 1973

By 1973, after four Python years, the team had established themselves in the UK as a comedy institution. No longer a cult, their third series had attracted a regular audience of over nine million and had won Best Light Entertainment Programme at the British Screen Awards. A few months after the series concluded, the group had embarked on a sell-out live stage tour, playing to devoted fans across the UK and Canada, released the best-selling *Brand New Monty Python Bok* and recorded a new audio album, *Monty Python's Matching Tie and Handkerchief*. Incredibly, they had still had time to work on the script for a new movie, *Monty Python and the Holy Grail*, which would be filmed in the early summer of 1973.

All of which should have led to mounting anticipation for Series Four of *Flying Circus* – but there was a small issue. John Cleese, who had been writing sketch-based material for ten years, had become frustrated with the format. He had been a slightly reluctant participant in Series Three (claiming "Dennis Moore" and "Cheese Shop" only were totally original ideas), but remained loyal to the team. However, none of the Pythons were too surprised when he drew the line at writing or performing in another *Flying Circus* series. They were initially unsure about whether to continue without him, but gradually saw the move as an opportunity to develop a more unified show, each episode bound by a single narrative.

The BBC were more cautious, seemingly unwilling to trust the talent of the remaining five Pythons. In April 1974, they offered them just a six-part series, which would air on the "minority" channel BBC2 and distanced it from the *Flying Circus* by calling it simply *Monty Python*. They even tried to insist the group made a pilot episode, a suggestion the group found patronising and rejected out-of-hand.

The new shows dispensed with the scattergun sketch approach, replacing it with storylines featuring characters, including ballooning pioneers the Montgolfier Brothers and Mr Neutron, the most dangerous man in the world, and themes such as *Hamlet* or politics. But this did not prevent them from introducing typical Python concepts, such as "A Party Political Broadcast on Behalf of the Norwegian Party", "Mrs Gorilla and Mrs Non-Gorilla Discuss Shopping", "The Icelandic Honey Seller" and "The Batsmen of the Kalahari".

Above: Photograph from a publicity shoot for the fourth series of *Monty Python*.

Judged against the highs of the former series, the first couple of episodes disappointed many viewers and even the Pythons themselves, but they had their excuses. The lack of John as a writer was a hurdle they could negotiate, but they sorely missed him as a performer, particularly the sensible/silly brilliance with which he played the authority roles. They also put themselves under greater pressure than ever. They had just expended great effort writing the *Holy Grail* movie and now had to come up with ideas, write, shoot and edit the series. They didn't even have time to shuffle the broadcast order of the shows around as they had done in previous series. Terry G had created new opening credits and his animations remained consistently good, but lack of time severely limited the number he was able to contribute.

Although the series continued to attract around five million viewers, which was a good audience for BBC2, the press were initially lukewarm in their praise. Only with episode three, "The Light Entertainment War", did they admit that the Pythons hadn't lost their touch. Peter Purser, in the *Sunday Times*, claimed they were "back in cracking form" while in the *Observer*, Clive James wrote, "The pressure on the new Cleese-less team to be as good as ever has perhaps been a little fierce, but that's showbiz … Anyway, the laughs came and everybody relaxed…"

Peter Woods [a real-life newsreader]: "… *The Second World War has now entered a sentimental stage. This morning on the Ardennes Front, the Germans started spooning at dawn, but the British Fifth Army responded by gazing deep in their eyes, and the Germans are reported to have gone 'all coy'.*" "The Light Entertainment War", Series Four, episode 3

By the end of the series, there was a general feeling that *Flying Circus* had run its course, with the Pythons ready to move on to individual projects and promoting the forthcoming *Holy Grail* film. Indeed, in his diary, after a series of meetings with the group, Michael marks February 22, 1975 as "the day on which Python finally died". In 45 episodes over five years, they had created some of the most memorable TV comedy ever made. And, of course, Michael was wrong, Python couldn't die: there were growing numbers of fans around the world who would make sure that could never happen.

"One of the things about *Python* was that it was never as good as the last thing we did. The second series, people would say, "it's quite funny but not as good as the first." Then the third series, "Well, very funny but not as good as the second," *The Holy Grail*? Good, but not as good as the TV series." Terry Jones

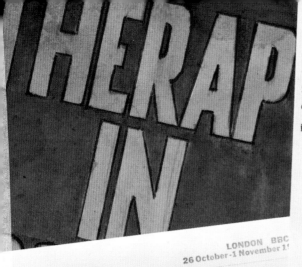

THERAP IN

Eating

Time Out May 4—10 1973 18

All restaurants reviewed provide food, except where stated. Prices quoted should not be taken as in any way indicative of prices actually charged, nor should the description of the restaurants be assumed to be in any way a description of the restaurants. Please let us know of any food you may have seen or been near recently.

● **The Vom-it**
7—9 North Circular, NW. 278 (a 7-hour walk)
Open 5 years a day.
Not licensed. Does not provide food of any sort, but Mr. & Mrs. Scrotum do their best to keep cheerful and encourage their customers to do the same. Help to while away the long hours by singing and talking about food. Plates are 2p and knives and forks 1p each.
● **Pukes**
Lower Bridge End Road Street, Barnet.

Open occasionally. 2.30 am—6.00 pm. Not really worth a walk, but o.k. if you happened to be in Barnet and unable to get out. Some of the dishes include food, and one of our inspectors found a lump of marinated dough stuck to the underside of his plate. Worth examining the table- and chair-seats, as either may well that extra portion.

Cafe
...Building Site, Dalston.
...12. (279 9678). Closed.
...d one. Probably the only
...d one in London. Friendly.
...lenty of chat. Hardly any dead
...d atmosphere. The tables may
...ffy, but if you're a regular here,
...will come and wipe them down
...wn cloth. If you're new, don't
...by the hostile glances, or the
...totally ignore you—it's well
...a glimpse of the food. Hard

to describe, but there's plenty of it. One plate of food: 5p. One mug of drink: 2p.
● **The Rita Room**
Further along, The Building Site, Dalston. Open 6—12 (278 3456). Closed weekdays. This one used to belong to the Rita Chain, but has been bought up by Charles Forte. All the same features as Rita's, plus a full orchestra and expensively mounted floor-show. Stars have included: Tom Jones and Englebert Humperdinck and the staff of the Encyclopedia Britannica answering questions on gardening. Not a place to be seen by the in-crowd. Entertainment, plate of food and use of lavatory: £50 inc.

Flash One

● **Carmello's**
261 Cheyney Walk, SW.1
Open 10.00 pm.—2.00 pm. (last orders 10.30
(first orders 10.15 pm.)
Really fantastic! They have food! And what's more they give you this food if you pay them! Absolutely sensational! Soup is rather an expensive starter (20p) but it's hot and it really is great! And the main

courses are
include me...
sauce (80p...
with potat...
knockout!...
world! So...
85p was ...
somethin...
over it fo...
I had to ...
good eve...
write it ...
the wall ...
Do you ...
coffee! ...
somet...
coffee ...
is coff...
Look ...
(The ...
subm...

● **LONDON BBC**
26 October—1 November 19

RadioTimes
...ython's flying

Were the Montgolfier brothers the first balloonists? Was Louis XIV a Glaswegian? Should you vote Norwegian at the next election? Answers to these and other silly questions in Monty Python, Thursday BBC2 Colour Page 6: Who are these people, anyway?

"THIS IS MY PSYCHIATRIC CLUB TIE, AND AS YOU CAN SEE THE CUFFLINKS MATCH. I'VE GOT A COPY OF *PSYCHIATRY TODAY* IN MY BAG, WHICH I THINK IS PRETTY CONVINCING. AND A LETTER HERE FROM MY MOTHER IN WHICH SHE ASKS HOW THE PSYCHIATRY IS GOING..." "BOGUS PSYCHIATRISTS", "HAMLET", SERIES FOUR, EPISODE 5

OLONIC IRRIGATION

"... YOU SAID YOU'D CLEAN THE TIGER OUT, BUT DO YOU? NO. I SUPPOSE YOU'VE LOST INTEREST IN IT NOW. NOW IT'LL BE ANT ANT ANT FOR A COUPLE OF DAYS, THEN ALL OF A SUDDEN, 'OH, MUM, I'VE BOUGHT A SLOTH' OR SOME OTHER ODD-TOED UNGULATE LIKE A TAPIR." "BUYING AN ANT", "MICHAEL ELLIS" SERIES FOUR, EPISODE 2

Film

CENSORED

'Aardvark' Hendon Classic. Till yesterday.

● **Hendon Classic**
'Aardvark': a rare and moving glimpse of a rare and moving animal. Till yesterday.
● **Gospel Oak Odeon**
'The Weather Forecast' (X) Graham Parker, Bert Foord. At last, the film of the success-ful BBC series. It's all there including the classic 'fog warning' and 'that's all from us till tomorrow, goodnight.' Some of the material has dated, but it's worth it for the superb rape scene.
● **Grays Inn Road Bioscope**
'Time Out at St. Trinian's': the film of the successful magazine. Mass self-abuse session shot at Harrow. Showing with 'Look at Life' No 48: Philip Jenkinson.
● **Playmate Cinema**
'Victor Lowndes Presents' (from midnight). The film of the millionaire (90 mins). The credit sequence is a little long (80 mins) but the rest of the film is nice and short.
● **Low Grade Cinema** (Ttnhm. Ct. Rd.)
'The Osmonds Live at the White House': Watch the Nixons go wild! Tricia whipping herself into delirium, Pat positively writhing, even Richard is on his chair, cheering these great entertainers, by the end. Showing with 'Look at Life' No 176: Napalm.
● **Biograph**
The National Film Board of Canada presents **'Another Look at New Zealand'** (140 mins). Almost all of New Zealand is in this. + The New Zealand Film Board's award-winning **'Hello Canada'**: the slow-moving story of the Canadian countryside. It's been severely cut by its distributors from its original 3 hours to 7 minutes. Still too long.
● **ICA**
'Robert Having his Other Nipple Pierced' The sequel. This one features Mike Parkinson and introduces Nicholas Parsons to him. + **'4th Girl Required to Share'**: Not a film. A small ad. Go anyway. + **'Carry On Robert Having His Nipple Pierced'**: the usual crowd in the usual jokes.
● **Casino**
'McWhiter Bros.': How the West End was won. A moving story about a couple of brothers and their desperate struggle for publicity.
● **St. Martin's Hospital**
'Buckets of Blood Pouring out of People's Heads': (for times see local press). A new Peckinpah. And none the more welcome for that. A loving and terribly honest look at some blood plasma.
● **Cineclub 24**
'Can I Have a Knighthood Please?': the new Richard Attenborough film. Richard directs this one with all the skill of a new-comer. An unusual story which suggest that the House of Windsor is directly descended from God. A...of Elizabeth I...

team of bombers (Barbara Windsor, Ch... Hawtrey, Joe Bugner) disguised as Sant... Claus (Kenneth Connor) hilariously des... large parts of South East Asia. 'A riot' (Evng. Nws.). + 'Ealing to Ongar' (last train 1.05): the film of the Central Line. Quite good.

● **Cannon Row Police Station**
'It's the Fuzz' (from Tuesday). The zany whacky world of the PC seen through the eyes of the Drug Squad. Great rape scene. Some police pubes. Weak on bristols. + **'Carry on Nazi'**: the usual crowd camping it up in Nazi Germany. Worth it for Peter Butterworth's Goering.
● **Turnpike Lane Launderama**
'Up the Plaster' (N. Sherrin). British comedy at its most persistent. This is Ned's fifth film and it's really time he learned. Script by David Frost, Neil Shand, Pius XII, Rod Laver and Karl Mildenburger etc. + 'Carry on Developing': the whacky ...

MR. NEUTRON

RAF BANTER

This is a two-and-a-half-minute skit in which Python show that they can still do traditional sketch comedy better than anyone before or since. In an episode with a rich seam of humour based on language and misunderstanding, this parody of British World War Two movies features Eric as Squadron Leader, Graham Chapman as Wingco and Terry Jones as the brilliantly named Squiffy Bovril.

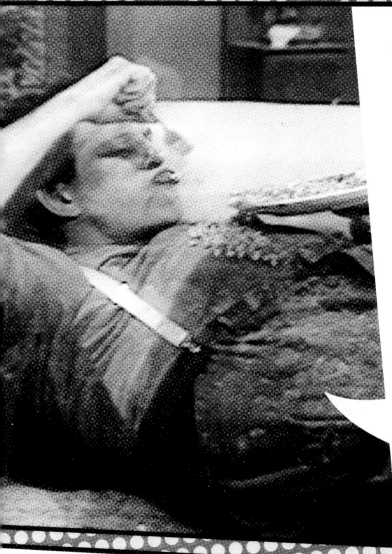

THE MOST AWFUL FAMILY IN BRITAIN

"Lady Organs: He's superb. His gobbing is consistent and accurate. His son is a dirty foul little creature, and those frightful scabs which Mrs Jodrell licks off the cat are …" "The Most Awful Family in Britain", *Series Four, episode 6*

The Garibaldi Family, holders of the East Midlands Most Awful Family (Lower Middle Class Division), might not have taken the national honour, registering only 15 on the disgustometer, but they are still held in great esteem by legions of Pythons fans.

Despite being, in many ways, a very un-Pythonesque sitcom-type sketch, the team effort pulls them through: Michael as the clumsy-to-destruction, Rhodesia-obsessed son; the tarty, PVC mini-skirted Member of Parliament daughter played by Graham; Terry J as a laxative-fixated dad; and Eric as the placid mother at the epicentre of the chaos, calmly ironing the telephone and the cat, and dealing with a Liberal candidate throwing kung-fu moves.

Missing from the list, of course, is Terry Gilliam. He would appear more frequently in the fourth series. "I really enjoyed the performances," he says. "I thought it was great to get out in front of the camera so that people knew what that animation guy looked like. I knew I wasn't as accomplished a performer as the others, but I really threw myself into my parts." Terry would give a memorable, if not subtle, performance as Kevin Garibaldi, lying on the couch with an overflowing plate of baked beans. Of all his roles, this was the one he most relished, saying, "I always enjoyed asking for more beans and being completely vile."

oody & Tinny Words

...ights of the English language bore more fruit in "The Light Entertainment War" episode with this fabulous...
...n the upper classes of the 1940s. Looking out on garden of their stately home and attended by their
...sque servants, Mansfield Vermin-Jones (Graham) his wife (Eric) and their daughter (Carol) discuss the
...ant or unpleasant sounds of various words. They savour the "woody words" and express disgust (the
...hter becoming quite distraught) at "tinny words". The sketch also stands out for one of Graham's finest
...rmances, as he relishes every syllable and loses himself in a litany of suggestive words:

...her: 'Sausage'! There's a good woody sort of word, 'sausage'. 'Gorn.'
...ghter: 'Antelope!'
...her: Where? On the lawn? [*He picks up a rifle*]
...ughter: No, no, Daddy. Just the word.
...ther: Don't want antelope nibbling the hoops.
...ughter: No, no – 'ant-e-lope'. Sort of nice and woody type of thing."
...Woody and Tinny Words", "The Light Entertainment War", Series Four, episode 3

Woody: Gorn, Sausage, Caribou, Intercourse, Pert, Thighs, Botty, Erogenous Zone, Concubine. Loose Woman, Ocelot, Wasp, Yowling

Tinny: Newspaper, Litter Bin, Leap, Tit, Simkins

Bit Tinny: Recidivist

THE LESSER SPOTTED PYTHON SCRIPT

THE BUDGETS FOR *MONTY PYTHON'S FLYING CIRCUS* WERE TIGHT AND VERY LITTLE MATERIAL WAS WASTED. THE PYTHONS WOULD RE-WRITE SCRIPTS THEY FELT DIDN'T QUITE WORK, SOMETIMES LETTING THE OTHER TEAM PLAY AROUND WITH THE IDEA, OR, AS ERIC SAID IN *THE PYTHONS AUTOBIOGRAPHY*, "IF WE THOUGHT IT WAS A BIT OLD OR HACKNEYED OR NOT VERY FUNNY WE'D JUST SEND IT TO THE TWO RONNIES, OR ROY HUDD."

By the time they reached the recording stage, the group was pretty sure that the sketches would be good enough for the show. Those that were shot were worked into a broadcast episode, even if they had to be fitted into a programme further down the series. However, there are some famous exceptions. The scripts of these are preserved in the Python archives and some of those scripts have been reproduced for this book (see front and back pockets.)

"WEE-WEE WINETASTING"

Probably the most notorious of all, this sketch was originally planned for episode 10, Series Three. Written by Eric and Michael, it is on the puerile side of Python – somewhat distasteful and pretty silly – but it's the kind of material many fans love. It was cut at the insistence of a nervous BBC management, but they did have the support of John, who said in the 1989 documentary *Life of Python* " … There was this sketch, and all the other Pythons thought it was pretty funny, and I didn't think it was funny enough to justify what I thought was the slight tackiness involved, and I remember that I found myself on the side of the establishment."

"COWARDLY BOXER"

This gem of a sketch was included in the script for episode 11 in Series One. It features Henry Pratt, a British light heavyweight boxer (due to be played by Graham), whose fighting style was marked by a remarkable sense of cowardice.

"THE COCKTAIL BAR"

This sketch featured three city gents (John, Terry J and Michael) discussing finance and ordering disgusting cocktails) in the Fox and Half-a-Bee pub. It was another victim of the BBC purge of Series Three, but was revived in some of the live shows, including *Live at Drury Lane*.

"MRS URSULA HITLER"

Originally scripted for the very last *Flying Circus* episode, this piece on Mrs Ursula Hitler, Britain's greatest beekeeper, never made it to broadcast.

Other shorter un-broadcast or un-shot pieces worthy of note include a censored Terry G animation apparently depicting Jesus on the cross, but which is revealed to be a telegraph pole being worked on by a telephone engineer; a sculptor played by Graham defending his statue of a mayor (John), which is perfect – apart from the inclusion of a ludicrously large nose; an opening scene set in the tunnel of Chelsea FC (one of the leading clubs of the time), which, so it's claimed, Eric was able to organize; and some amusing additional material to "The Deadliest Joke in the World" sketch.

The Monty Python contribution to *Euroshow 71*, an hour-long May Day special showcasing the best of European TV variety, was shown as part of the BBC's *Python Night* in 1999. In the six-minute film, John Cleese narrates an increasingly silly digest of British May Day traditions – which include the Gavotte of the Long John Silvers, Nun-Boiling Week and the Spring Dance of the Futures Brokers – while noting, "In Hereford, nothing happens at all." This piece would also feature the original footage of "The Fish-Slapping Dance" and the Batley Women's Institute mud-fighting.

In those heady days of the early 1970s, while the team were writing and performing TV series, live shows, movies and records, they also found time to script and shoot corporate promotional films for companies to use to motivate their sales reps and staff. These included a six-minute "Close-Up Toothpaste Advert", a "Harmony Hairspray" short and a 25-minute classic entitled "The Great Birds Eye Peas Relaunch of 1971". These are classic Python pieces, complete with fabulous Pepperpots, a Gumby, Eric as the Comparatively Good Fairy ("Well nobody's perfect!") and voices of authority from John and Graham.

"In Bolton, Lancashire, May Day means the Annual Return of the Overdue Library Book - a much-loved ceremony that somehow captures the spirit of all that is most colourful, exciting and indeed, exotic in the North of England."

Euroshow 71, May Day special

"I remember the lady at the sweetshop, she copped one in January ... There was a good rude one in March, which caused a lot of trouble in the Wandsworth area."

Additional material for "The Deadliest Joke in the World"

"This is the story they said was too uninteresting to be made. A stirring tale of heroism, of courage and of selfless devotion in the service of the frozen vegetable trade." "The Great Birds Eye Peas Relaunch of 1971"

"In the dark days of '42 we were really up against it. The chaps in my squadron were reduced to keeping their hair in place with low-grade engine oil. It got your fingers all greasy, headsets kept slipping and, well, frankly, the chaps wouldn't look at you in the mess. Which was why we were so bally pleased when the boffins came up with new Harmony Hairspray. So now one of the top tacticians of new Harmony, the chap who came up the specifications of the bouncing hairspray which demolished the German hairdressers, Nurse, now Chief Test Pilot Dennis Karslake, he's going to put it in a nutshell."

Biggles (John Cleese), "Harmony Hairspray" relaunch promotional film, 1973

ACTION	SOUND

SCENE 20. FILM.

(CUT TO WEMBLEY CROWD CHEERING).

SCENE 21.

(CUT TO TWO SHOT OF TWO ON
INTERVIEW CHAIRS. (DIFFERENT SET,
ALAS ONE OF THEM IS BEHAVING
PUNCHILY).

V/O.
And now boxing. A close look at

the new British Light Heavyweight

Prospect Henry Pratt who has taken

the world of Boxing by storm.

(SLIGHT PAUSE AND THE PUNCH DRUNK
PERSON REVEALS HE'S THE INTERVIEWER.)

PUNCHY.
Henry - you've taken the world of

boxing by storm.

HENRY.
Yes I have. Ha ha har...

-21-

PUNCHY.
Henry you've had fourteen
professional fights so far and none
of them has yet gone beyond Round
One.

HENRY.
Absolutely right.

PUNCHY.
Well this is remarkable, what would
you put it down to?

HENRY.
Sheer lack of ability allied with
extreme physical cowardice.

PUNCHY.
And yet in your first month you've
had fourteen fights.

HENRY.
Well people like my style, I've
got personality. There's the ring
bathed in floodlights, trumpets
going like billy-oh, hush falls
over the crowd, bell goes...whoosh.
Clean pair of heels, nowhere to be
seen, straight up into the bar....
nice cold lager. Not a scar,
Fight after fight. Doesn't take
anything out of me.

PUNCHY.
Well what first gave you the idea?

HENRY.
Well I think I had the idea in
the Army. I was frightfully good
at running away from things.
Whoosh, clean pair of heels.
Didn't matter what lamp-posts,
shopping bag, old ladies, you
name it I ran away from it.
I thought to myself here's a
gimmick. When I'm up in that
ring for those fleeting seconds,
two things happen. First the
working classes, and I'm not
saying a word against them,
do enjoy seeing a cowardly
guards officer being chased out
of a ring by one of their own
kind.

This previously unpublished section of "Ursula Hitler" was cut from the very last episode of Monty Python's Flying Circus.

(LINKMAN ON PIER AT PAIGNTON.

SMALLISH CROWD BEHIND HIM INCLUDING JEREMY THORPE WHO WAVES AT CAMERA FROM THE BACK)

LINKMAN.
Hello and welcome to Paignton,

because it's _from_ Paignton that

we're going back to the studio.

Michael: *well we're already here · so let's go over there*

(CUT BACK TO THE NEWSREADER).

Graham: *Hello, ~~from we to~~ this here we go over there.*

NEWSREADER.
Welcome back. And now it's time

for part 8 of our series about the

life and work of Ursula Hitler,

the Surrey housewife who revolutionised

British bee-keeping in the 1930s.

(GENTLE MUSIC.)

(MIX TO MONTAGE OF FADED 1920s STYLE
PHOTOS IN BLACK AND WHITE OR SEPIA —
PERHAPS TERRY G. COULD MAKE THEM UP.
MOSTLY OF A NICE LADY WITH NET OVER
HER HEAD POSING AMONGST HER HIVES IN
A GENTEEL GARDEN. POSING WITH OTHER
APIARISTS. DOING THINGS TO HIVES ETC.
ONE STILL IN THE MIDDLE OF THESE SHOWS
HER IN A BIG FISH MARKET OR
INDUSTRIAL FISH-CURING FACTORY HOLDING
A BIG FISH.)

CAPTION: URSULA HITLER. BRITAIN'S
              GREATEST APIARIST.

CAPTION 2. PART FOUR: THE DIFFICULT
              YEARS.

CAMS	ACTION	SOUND

V.O.

Born plain Ursula Lloyd-George, in North Wales in 1897, she had changed her name to Baldwin in 1922 to avoid publicity. But when Stanley Baldwin became Prime Minister in 1923, she was forced to change it again, being briefly Mrs. Doris Ramsey McDonald and Mrs. Ursula Hoare-Belisha, before becoming Mrs. Ursula Hitler in 1934. But her bee-keeping had suffered from years of insecurity and confusion. Parts for the hive were still arriving under the name Baldwin and being sent back by Mrs. Hitler's assistant, Miss Roosevelt, under the mistaken impression that she was still Miss Hoare-Belisha.

CUT TO.

(FILM, PRESENT DAY. AN APIARY. A DEAR OLD LADY IS ROVING AROUND THE APIARY TALKING TO CAMERA. AT BOTTOM OF HIVES A LITTLE HOLE MARKED "BEES ONLY")

CAMS	ACTION	SOUND

MISS HITLER.
I well remember in September
1939 I was out at the hives,
de-coning the Queen, when the
postman...

(QUICK CUT TO PEPPERPOT DRESSED
AS A POSTMAN)

...brought me a letter from
Whitehall saying that if I did
not withdraw my troops from Poland
before midnight I would be in a
state of war with Britain...well
of course I threw the letter away
and Europe was immediately plunged
into a bloody imbroglio which
lasted 6 bitter years, and unleashed
social economic changes, which
swept away the last crumbling vestiges
of the Western imperialist hegenony.

CUT TO:

(INTERVIEWER, A SHERIDAN MORLEY
TYPE)

INT.
Yes...yes...of course, but...

(WE NOTICE THAT HE IS HOLDING A GUN,
POINTED AT MRS. HITLER)

How did this affect the beekeeping?

CAMS	ACTION	SOUND

MRS.HITLER.
The fighting?

INT.
No...no the beekeeping...how
was it affected in the war years?
were the hives disrupted?...I
expect supplies were difficult..

MRS.HITLER.
Well, there were marked changes
certainly - the tench became
shorter...and the grippies who'd
normally breed anywhere, developed
a lot of fish-mould....so obviously
I couldn't keep them in the same
hives as the trout - or else the
trout would have been affected.

INT.
In 1946, as Mrs. Sir Stafford
Cripps, you introduced a
revolutionary new concept into
beekeeping.

MRS.HITLER.
Yes, I did. I marked each of them
with a tiny red mark and then
dropped them into the pool. (INTERVIEWER
LOOKS PUZZLED) This enabled us to
restock the salmon grounds which

- 56 -

/CONTD. ...

CAMS	ACTION	SOUND

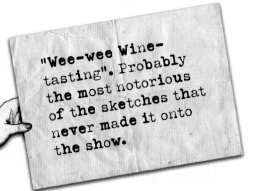

"Wee-wee Wine-tasting". Probably the most notorious of the sketches that never made it onto the show.

BIG C.U. OF AN ANNOUNCER.

ANNOUNCER:
That was the third in a series

of programmes in which we examine

our moral beliefs. Later this

evening...(REACTS TO A NOISE)

...ooh, I'd better go, someone's

coming.

(HE CLIMBS INTO A BARREL
BESIDE HIM AND LOWERS THE
LID DOWN. PULL OUT TO
REVEAL THAT THE BARREL IS ONE OF
A ROW OF BARRELS IN THE CHATEAUX
CELLARS A FRENCHMAN, M.Hounslow

West, WALKS ALONG WITH AN
ARISTOCRATIC ENGLISH WINE MERCHANT,
Mr. West Ruislip for Ickenham.

M. Hounslow West taps a barrel
and gives a glass to Mr. West
Ruislip for Ickenham)

M.H.W.:
How about this, sir?

MR. W.R.F.I.:
(TASTING ELABORATELY)...'Mm...

it's a slightly flinty breed...

sharp and resolute, with a terse smokiness

in the aftertaste...is it a Pouilly

Fume...?

M.H.W.:
No, it's wee-wee.

MR. W.R.F.I.:
Ah yes!

M.H.W.:
(MOVING ON TO ANOTHER BARREL AND
TAPPING IT) Try this one, M'sieur...

MR. W.R.F.I:
(TASTING ELABORATELY AGAIN)...
'Mm...now...I must be careful
here...this is very vigorous..
again lively neat and sharp...
oh but what a finish...yes...I
think I know this one...yes...
is it a Moselle?

M.H.W.:
No, sir...it's wee-wee again.

MR. W.R.F.I.:
Ohdear...you got me again.

- 55 -

(M. HOUNSLW WEST OFFERS
HIM ANOTHER GLASS FROM A
DIFFERENT BARREL)

M.H.W.:
One more here, sir.

(MR. WEST RUISLIP FOR ICKENHAM
TASTES IT)

MR. W.R.F.I.:
Ah...Ah yes...yes...no

mistaking this, this definitely

is...er...~~is wee-wee~~, isn't it.

M.H.W.:
Yes it's wee-wee again.

MR.W.R.F.I.:
Well, I've got a lot to learn..

M.H.W.:
It has taken me many years to

lay down these silly things.

It is my life's work...this

and baby-sitting.

MR. W.R.F.I.:
Baby-sitting?

M.H.W.:
Yes, sir, I love it.

MR. W.R.F.I.:
Well my wife and I are going

out on Thursday to see Oldham

Athletic at the Talk of The Town,

could you help us out?

M.H.W.:
Certainly sir...I'll be round

about 7.30

MR. W.R.F.I.:
Lovely...

Right well ... hold ...

(THEY WALK OFF CHATTING. WE
STAY ON THE BARRELS. A LID
OPENS AND THE ANNOUNCER, SODDEN WITH
WHATEVER WAS IN THE BARREL, LOOKS
OUR FURTIVELY)

ANNOUNCER:
The next sketch follows after some silly

noises.

(HE DUCKS BACK IN THE BARREL.
CUT TO BLACK HALF A MINUTE OF
VERY SILLY NOISES. GILLIAM
SHOULD BE CONSULTED HERE AS
HE CAN MAKE MORE SILLY NOISES
THAN ANYONE I KNOW, APART FROM
MY MOTHER.

ANYWAY, THESE SILLY NOISES
GRADUALLY RESOLVE INTO CHURCH
BELLS PEELING AND STILL OF A
PARISH CURCH IS FADED IN.)

THE FLYING CIRCUS IN AMERICA

"I THINK AMERICAN FANS HAVE ALWAYS BEEN MORE DEVOTED – 'FANATICAL' IS A GOOD WORD. PEOPLE WHO DISCOVERED PYTHON FELT THEY HAD MADE A MAJOR DISCOVERY." NANCY LEWIS, US PUBLICIST

Monty Python's Flying Circus would never take off in the United States. That was the view of the US rights holders Time-Life, it was the opinion of American TV execs and it was even the belief of the Pythons themselves. They might all have been proved right if it hadn't been for the efforts of a couple of true believers.

Nancy Lewis was a New York publicist and in 1972 she was working for the company distributing the Pythons records in the States. Her approach was to promote the group to FM radio stations as if they were an English rock group – a concept welcomed by American college students already weaned on the Beatles, the Who and Led Zeppelin. Plugging the records and using *And Now For Something Completely Different*, a film based on re-shot sketches from Series One and Two, as a promotional tool, she started to build a cult following for the group across the country.

As the Python's tour of Canada in 1973 drew to a close, Nancy flew up to meet them and persuaded all the team except John to fly down to California to do some promotion. They were given a 30-minute spot on *The Tonight Show*, which bombed completely, and then performed some better-received sketches on *Midnight Special*.

"We were supposed to do 30 minutes' material live on *The Tonight Show* with Joey Bishop. He introduced us, saying, "Here's some guys from England, people tell me they're funny..." We started doing a Pepperpots sketch and looked out at the audience – it was like *The Producers* – staring with their jaws wide open. We did the 30 minutes [of] material in 15 minutes flat to no laughter whatsoever." Eric Idle

Around this time, Ron Devillier enters the story. Ron was Vice-President of Programming for KERA, a PBS station in Dallas, when a friend at Time-Life Films sent him a few episodes of *Flying Circus*, a series they had given up hope on and were considering bulk-erasing. Ron was captivated, eventually watching the whole 13 episodes in one sitting.

By the first Sunday in October 1974, Ron had *Monty Python's Flying Circus* on air in Dallas. It was soon breaking KERA's record audience figures. The series took off like a forest fire across the States; within six months, over 100 PBS stations (including Chicago, New York, Boston and Philadelphia) had picked up the show. In the spring of 1975, the Pythons (minus John),

on a promotional tour for *Monty Python and the Holy Grail*, visited the station. There, they were questioned live on air by a young audience and Ron himself. A surviving 13-minute clip of the interview is available on YouTube.

If Python was to be a success in the USA, it could only have been through PBS. Only the publicly funded stations were brave and independent-minded enough to put the show on – and could broadcast *Flying Circus* uninterrupted by adverts. However, with Python fever engulfing the country, the commercial networks wanted some of the action.

In April 1975, the five remaining Pythons appeared as co-hosts on ABC's new breakfast show (also available on YouTube), being affable and silly in between reports from Vietnam on the fall of Saigon. As they acted up over the closing credits, playfully "destroying" the studio, they were unaware they were about to face real conflict with the station.

Instead of selling the shows to PBS, Series Four of *Flying Circus* had been sold to ABC. The network then edited this into two 45-minute shows for its series *ABC's Wide World of Entertainment*. When the Pythons saw the intended programmes they were stunned. In order to edit the shows to fit and to create ad breaks, anything remotely risqué, any nudity,

single words such as "God", "Hell" and "Damn", and even the words "naughty bits", had been cut! The result was a discordant shambles and an insult to the meticulous, creative way the shows had been assembled.

Failing in their attempts to get the BBC to halt the sale or for ABC to compromise, the Pythons went legal on them. The two Terrys were key. As an American citizen, Terry G was able to take the case to an American court and, as they prepared it, lawyers discovered a clause that Terry J had inserted into their BBC contract, saying their material couldn't be cut without permission.

Once the court was shown both cut and uncut versions there was no contest. The judge felt it was too late to prevent broadcast, but found for the Pythons. It proved a landmark case in terms of US rights' ownership and, as a direct result, Monty Python would retain all overseas rights to *Flying Circus* from that point onwards. They sold the full episodes of Series Four to PBS.

Flying Circus was by now attracting a combined audience of around ten million viewers on PBS. While not comparable to networked hits, it was a groundswell of support that enabled the Pythons' first actual feature-length film, *Monty Python and the Holy Grail*, to achieve box-office success.

"When people heard it was coming on TV, it was something they knew from FM radio. The timing was brilliant. People over here like Elton John and Led Zeppelin were behind the show. Elton John was doing Python lines on stage! Zeppelin were talking about Python to everyone they met." Nancy Lewis, US publicist, *Mojo*

CANADA

1973

NORTH OF THE BORDER, CANADA HAD ALREADY TAKEN THE PYTHONS TO THEIR HEART. THE CANADIAN BROADCASTING CORPORATION (CBC) RAN THE FIRST *FLYING CIRCUS* SERIES IN THE AUTUMN OF 1970, JUST A YEAR AFTER ITS BRITISH TRANSMISSION. THEY PROCEEDED TO RUN THE SECOND SERIES STRAIGHT AWAY, BUT AFTER THE CHRISTMAS BREAK, AND VIEWERS WATCHING AN EARNEST SCIENCE PROGRAMME NAMED *THE WORLD WE LIVE IN* GRADUALLY REALIZED IT WAS NOT A PYTHON SKETCH, BUT A REPLACEMENT SHOW.

Outside CBC's Montreal studios, 150 people assembled to demonstrate the depth of their disgruntlement and support for the show. The broadcaster, shocked at the reaction, promised to air the rest of the series as soon as it could, and it was no surprise that, a year later, after the *And Now For Something Completely Different* movie broke box-office records in the country, the Pythons chose Canada for their first overseas stage tour.

CBC, now fully appreciative of the group, heralded their arrival in the country. It orchestrated a Beatlemania-style welcome, announcing the time of their next-day arrival at the airport, printing a four-page news sheet called *The Flying Python* and Gumby T-shirts, and providing an open-top bus to take the Pythons away from the small but vocal throng at the airport.

"When we arrived off the plane, there was a huge cheer and a couple of hundred fans. I looked behind me as I thought there must be some rock-and-roll band coming in too!" Eric Idle

The almost sell-out tour confirmed the group's affection for Canada and, despite the dubious habits the Pythons attributed to the nation's beloved Mounties, the country has provided a bedrock of support for the Pythons and welcomes them all back with open arms.

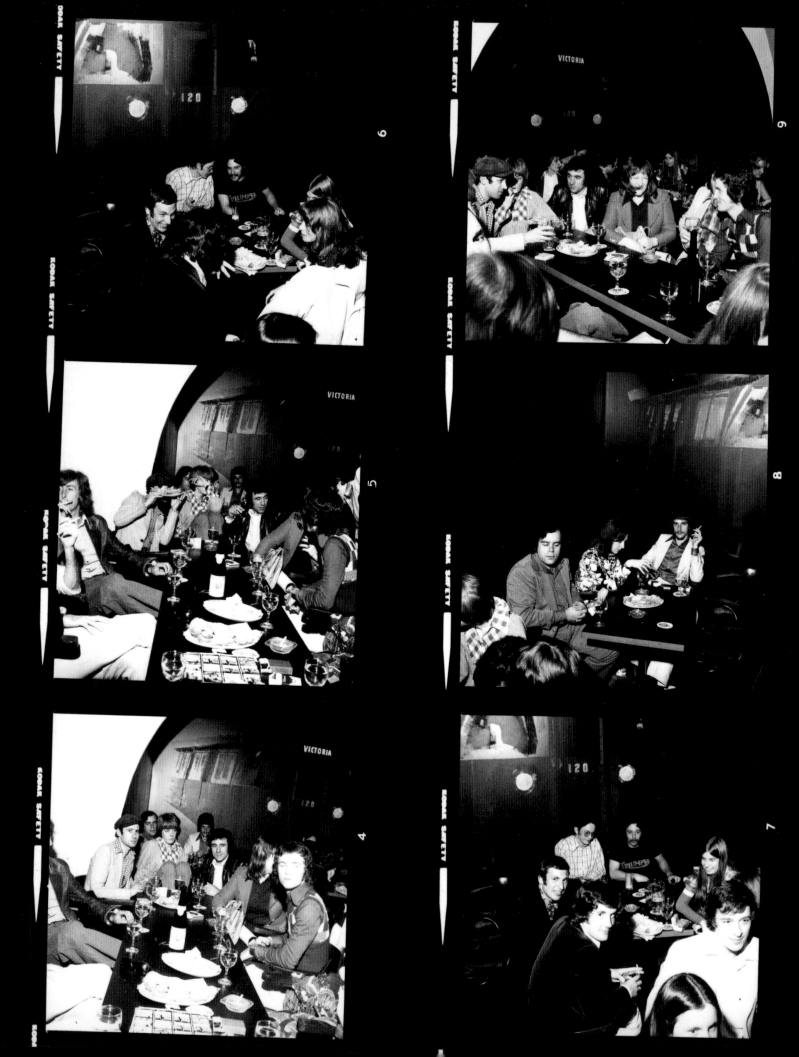

The First Farewell Tour

"**N**one of them knew what they were getting into and neither did I. We were all making it up as we went along." Tony Smith, road manager

The Pythons had always relished the performing side of their work. Having started out acting in their own sketches in revues, they had never really stopped. The studio portions of *Flying Circus* were recorded as live as possible in front of an audience; the first album was recorded as a live show at the Camden Theatre (now named Koko); and various combinations of the group would occasionally perform cabaret in small venues.

As early as June 1970, most of them appeared together at St Pancras Town Hall in London, as part of *Oh Hampstead*, a benefit for Ben Whitaker, the recently defeated Labour MP for Hampstead. Michael Palin's diaries recall that he and John performed the "Parrot Sketch" and Graham and Terry did "The Minister Whose Legs Fall Off".

At the very end of January 1971, Monty Python staged their first full live show, which took place in the slightly unlikely location of the Belgrade Theatre in Coventry, as part of the Lanchester Arts Festival. It was Eric's idea – he had made some occasional solo performances in the Midlands city – and he assembled the sketches, arranged the scant set and directed the show.

"**The first evening was a total smash, helped no doubt by the fact that we went on after midnight. The audience was loud and raucous and drunk as skunks. We had peaked at just the right moment. We were comedy gods to these kids who had never seen us live. The laughter was loud and long and the applause deafening.**" Eric Idle

The audience reaction to the three Coventry shows shocked the group. The crowds had been ecstatic, roaring with laughter, shouting enthusiastically over some performances and even refusing to leave until told to do so by John in his most threatening tone. There was a future in the live show game …

When the next shows came, in 1973, it was in the form of a rock-and-roll tour: two months on the road, 13 cities and 30 shows. Named the *First Farewell Tour*, the group, along with Carol Cleveland and Neil Innes, played the provincial cities of Britain; from Southampton to Norwich via Glasgow.

"**It was actually very refreshing. I didn't have to get any hotel rooms repaired. I had one or two libraries we had to redecorate, but other than that it was great.**" Tony Smith, road manager

There were a few problems, such as getting the sound right and Graham's excessive drinking, which caused him to arrive on stage late or sometimes not at all, but they were all having a ball. Graham and Terry J indulged in a competition over who could put on the silliest Pepperpot lipstick, while Michael celebrated his 30th birthday in Birmingham. Eric's mum, believed by an aghast audience and some gullible newspaper reporters to be TV morality campaigner Mary Whitehouse, came on stage and presented him with a cake. Michael then went into the "Gumby Flower Arranging" routine and plunged his chrysanthemums into the cake. "It was the most unforgettable birthday of my life," he said, "and one of the best times on stage with the Pythons."

Up and down the country, they played to generally full theatres, who enthusiastically greeted the characters they had recently seen on TV. They lapped up the "Llama Sketch", "Gumbys", "Nudge Nudge", "Pepperpots" and, of course, the "Parrot" sketch as well as old revue favourites including "Custard Pie" and "One Man Wrestling". Although the future of *Monty Python's Flying Circus* was in doubt (they had yet to commit to Series Four), *Monty Python Live* was up and kicking …

"**I remember the flight to Canada – First Class! A lounge behind the cockpit where you could drink and have a party – we were in love with being rock stars.**" Terry Gilliam

Having conquered Britain, the Pythons did what any self-respecting rock band would do and looked for new territories to win over. Canada, which had taken to Python more than anywhere else, was an obvious choice. The tour zig-zagged across the country, visiting major Canadian cities, but also some far-flung destinations.

"**Air Canada was on strike, a go-slow. The only thing it affected was our set. It was always a day or two behind us.**" Eric Idle

The Canadians flocked to the shows and, even in French Canada, got what the Pythons were doing. At the Winnipeg show, the whole front row came dressed as a caterpillar. For their part, the Pythons participated enthusiastically in the fun, creating anarchy on their TV appearances and joining in promotional gimmicks, such as being incarcerated in a giant cage, like quarantined animals, at Vancouver Airport. They were still lads and, although John had announced on the way to Vancouver that he was leaving the Flying Circus, for the others, who were set to fly down to LA for promotional appearances in the States, the party was still in full flow.

Monty Python promotional postcards featuring original Terry Gilliam artwork from Monty Python's Flying Circus.

MONTY PYTHON'S FLYING CIRCUS

back soon!

Live at Drury Lane, London, 1974

"I think I should add that some parts of the show are just a little bit shocking and obviously on the stage the cast can get away with more than they can on the BBC. But all in all that was really a night to remember." David Bowie, *Mirabelle Magazine*, 1974

In March 1974, although they were busy completing the *Holy Grail* script, the Pythons finally brought their live show home to London. For four weeks, extended from two due to demand, the opulent Theatre Royal, Drury Lane, in London's West End, hosted a programme of largely familiar sketches from the group. Over 2,000 fans - every night was a sell-out - packed the theatre, including show business royalty such as Mick Jagger, David Bowie, Pink Floyd and Elton John.

"I vividly remember going to see *Monty Python Live* at the Drury Lane theatre in 1974. It was one of the best nights of my young life. There they were, up on stage, right in front of me, my heroes, the most important thing in my world." Charlie Higson, writer

It was, of course, comedy as rock-and-roll. The audience, familiar with the sketches from the audio albums, burst into applause at the entrance of a recognisable figure, such as the Colonel or Praline, or the first few words of their favourite sketch, just as they would do for a band striking the first chords of a hit song. However, as John noted, they then subsided into silence. It took a stagehand to show him, from the wings, that they were mouthing the words. It was like a rock concert. The audience knew the sketches and had come to celebrate them with the Pythons.

For the first and only time, the team was missing Carol Cleveland, who was already booked on a European stage tour. Her place was taken by Eric's wife, Lyn Ashley, and Neil Innes augmented the group by appearing in some sketches. By now the favourites - "Silly Walks", the *"Parrot" sketch*, "Argument Clinic", "Cheese Shop", "Albatross", "Lumberjack", "Nudge Nudge" - were established. Knowing them inside out, as they did, the Pythons would attempt to catch each other out by changing lines, try to get one another to corpse and compete over silly made-up names, Graham trumping everyone with "Madame Emission Nocturnelle".

The set included their usual pre-Python material - "One-Man Wrestling" sketch and the "Custard Pie Lecture" - and a new "oldie", "The Four Yorkshiremen" from *At Last the 1948 Show*. This featured old men's competitive nostalgia for their increasingly ludicrous poverty-stricken childhoods, and it would become an eagerly anticipated element of Python live shows and Amnesty International charity performances.

The night also included a version of "Election Night Special" (very topical as the General Election had taken place just weeks before), "The Philosophers' Song", Eric Idle taking on the vocals of the "Lumberjack Song" and Neil Innes performing the Bonzo Dog Doo Dah Band song "How Sweet to be an Idiot".

Material new to the British audience included a "Secret Service Interview" sketch ("Interviewer: Can you keep a secret? Mr Leyton: Yes. Interviewer: Good, well you're in then..."), a mandolin-wielding Terry Gilliam hanging from wires singing "I've Got Two Legs" but being shot down before the second verse, and a version of the "Revolting Cocktail" sketch that was cut from Series Three of *Flying Circus*.

John: Oh, I say, have you seen page eight? Nixon's had an asshole transplant.
Terry: Ohhh, have you seen the stop press then?
John: No.
Terry: The asshole has rejected him.
Graham: Er, would you like a twist of lemming sir?
Terry: Oh ... yes please, Harry.
Graham: A bit more, sir?
Terry: Just a squeeze.
Graham: There you are, sir.
John: Alex, what will you have?
Michael: Oh, ahhh, Mallard Fizz for me please, Maurice."

The Drury Lane season was a triumph for the Pythons. The press were enthusiastic and the fans rapturous. The *New Musical Express* gave away a flimsy record (*Monty Python's Tiny Black Round Thing*), with excerpts from the show and a live album was released, which reached number 26 and stayed in the UK album charts all summer. But events were moving quickly - within weeks the Pythons were filming *Holy Grail* and writing Series Four of *Flying Circus*. It would be another 40 years before a Monty Python show was staged in the UK.

"For aficionados (I am one) the evening was one of almost uninterrupted enjoyment." B.A. Young, *Financial Times*

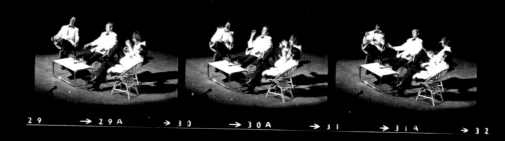

29 → 29A → 30 → 30A → 31 → 31A → 32

→ 19 → 19A → 20 → 20A → 21 → 21A → 22 → 22A → 23 → 23A

12A → 00 → 00A → 0 → 0A → 1 → 1A → 2 →

→ 36 → 36A → 37 → 37A → 38 → 38A → 39 → 39A → 40

→ 38 → 38A → 39 → 39A → 40 → 40A → 41 → 41A → 42 →

→ 24A → 25 → 25A → 26 → 26A → 27 → 27A → 28 → 28A

Python fever struck New York City in Easter 1976. On that side of the Atlantic, the group were at the peak of their popularity – *Flying Circus* was in its third year of US syndication and *Holy Grail* was a box-office smash. Excitement mounted as Monty Python were booked in at the 2,000-or-so-seater theatre in downtown Manhattan for a three-week stint of matinee and evening performances. The fans crowded the stage doors for a glimpse of their heroes. Various A-listers, Paul Simon, Keith Moon, Leonard Bernstein and Julie Andrews among them, laughed uncontrollably in the audience, while a modest George Harrison and an unsteady Harry Nilsson dressed as Canadian Mounties to join the "Lumberjack Song" chorus line. The show itself was based on the Drury Lane set, but adapted for US tastes. Sketches such as "Cocktail Bar" and "Election Night" were dropped, while "Blackmail" was added with new-to-theatre "Salvation Fuzz", "Crunchy Frog" and an amalgamation of Python courtroom sketches.

MONTYPYTHON

LIVE AT CITY CENTRE
NEW YORK, 1976

★★★★★

"PEOPLE SEEMED TO KNOW THE SKETCHES WELL AND THEY WHOOPED AND THEY WAILED AND THEY WERE DRESSED AS GUMBYS AND ALL SORTS OF STRANGE CHARACTERS AND WE COULD HARDLY GET A WORD OUT. WE COULDN'T HEAR OURSELVES. I'D NEVER EXPERIENCED ANYTHING LIKE THAT. I DON'T BELIEVE THE GUYS HAD EITHER AND THAT WAS THE FIRST TIME I THOUGHT, WOW, YES, WE MADE IT IN AMERICA. THIS IS EXCITING."

CAROL CLEVELAND

★★★★★

JOHN: "I'M WATCHING NOW FOR SOME OF THE STARS WHO WILL BE ATTENDING TONIGHT'S PERFORMANCE: CHARLTON HESTON, BARBRA STREISAND, SHIRLEY MACLAINE, STEVE MCQUEEN, ALI MCGRAW AND PAUL NEWMAN ARE AMONGST THOSE WHO CAN'T BE HERE TONIGHT, BUT THERE'S STILL A GALAXY OF BIG NAMES, A SHINING FIRMAMENT OF HUGE CELEBRITIES, A GLITTERING HOTS OF SUPERSTARS — ELIZABETH TAYLOR AND RICHARD BURTON, BUZZ ALDRIN, JACKIE ONASSIS AND PRESIDENT FORD — WHO HAVE SIMPLY REFUSED TO COME ..."

INTRODUCTION, MONTY PYTHON LIVE AT CITY CENTER, KING BISCUIT FLOWER HOUR RADIO SHOW, MAY 9, 1976

"They are vulgar, sophomoric, self-satisfied, literate, illiterate, charmless, crass, subtle and absolutely terrific. They are the funniest thing ever to come out of a television box ... The humor is occasionally raunchy, but for sheer irreverence, impertinence and spaced-out zaniness, there has been nothing to beat it since Genghis Khan." Clive Barnes, *New York Times*, April 1976

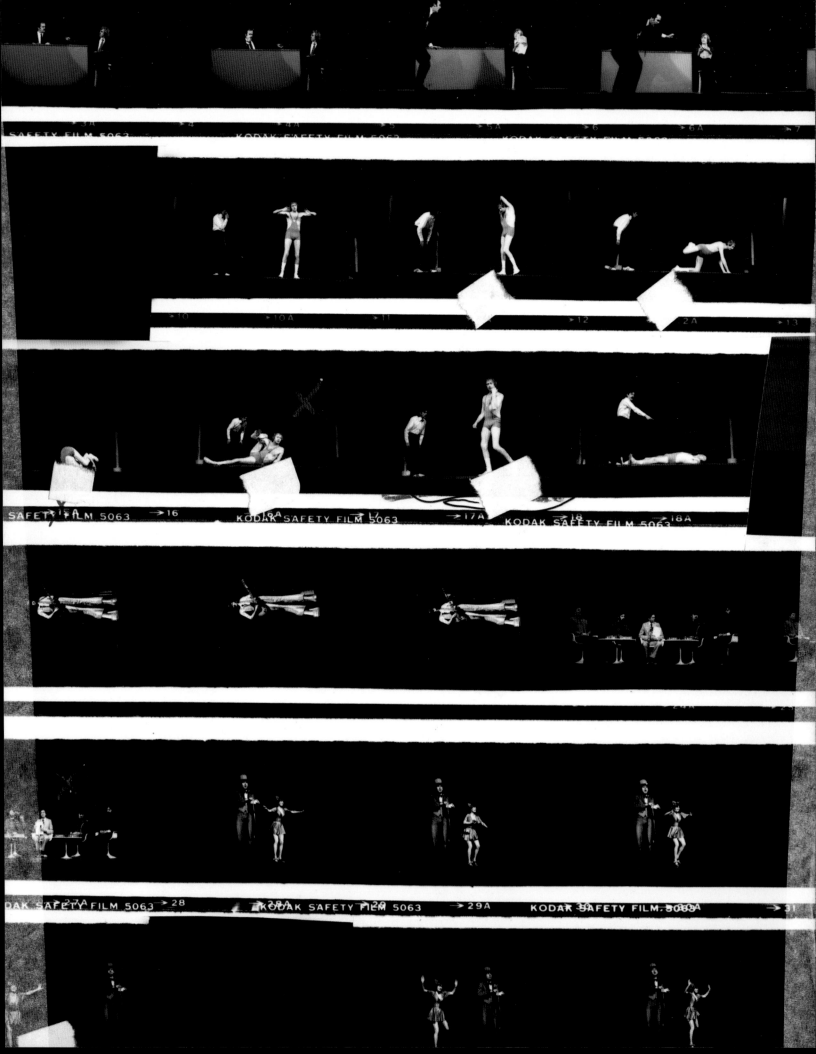

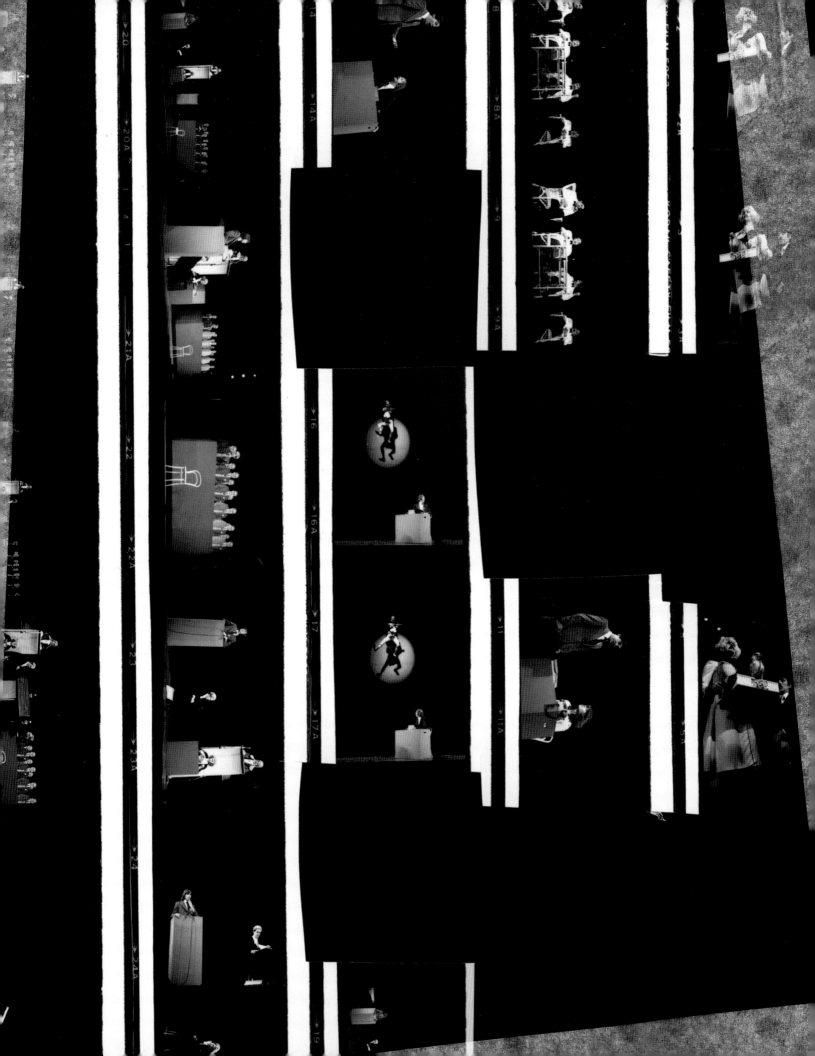

LIVE AT THE HOLLYWOOD BOWL, LOS ANGELES, 1980

WITH THEIR MOVIE MONTY PYTHON'S LIFE OF BRIAN A BOX-OFFICE TRIUMPH, THE PYTHON'S WERE READY FOR SOMETHING DIFFERENT - A LIVE SHOW UNDER THE STARS OF THE HOLLYWOOD SKY. A FABULOUS SUCCESS, THEY LEFT AUDIENCES AND PERFORMERS WITH MEMORIES THEY WOULD NEVER FORGET...

In 1980, the Python's were basking in the success of what many believed to be their greatest work, *Life of Brian*. Despite, or possibly helped by, controversy and religious opposition, the movie had been a staggering triumph, both critically and financially. So where better for a group of newly crowned film stars to head than Hollywood?

The arguments stacked up. They had yet to play the west coast of America, they were offered the gigantic Hollywood Bowl, where they could play to thousands in just a few performances, they had a ready-made and well-tuned set they could almost take off the shelf – and they were being offered a million dollars to do it (they never got it, but that's another story…) It was a no-brainer.

The Hollywood Bowl had been an iconic venue for decades. Mario Lanza, Frank Sinatra and Louis Armstrong had performed there, as well as pop bands such as the Doors and the Beatles. Although capable of accommodating twice as many, the Bowl could be easily transformed into an 8,000-seater venue, which was ideal for a four-night stint from the most famous comedy group in the entertainment capital of the world.

From the word go, this was always going to be a Python party; a joyous celebration of their work. The performers had nothing more to prove and could enjoy the rock-star adulation being showered on them. The September evenings were balmy and LA's Python fans obviously shared the relaxed vibe, arriving with their picnics, many of them dressed in character and more than a few with their own mood-enhancing stimulants.

Under the famous half-dome, massive projection screens were erected. As in the City Center shows, the set was to be enhanced by projected footage of Terry G's animations

> "It was kind of a party, because you sit in little boxes and everybody'd have their picnics out and everything like that and they're all smoking. I had to go out through the audience for the "Albatross" sketch and walk through all this marijuana smoke." **Terry Jones**

> "It's a typical Hollywood audience, Bruce. All the kids are on drugs and all the adults are on rollerskates."

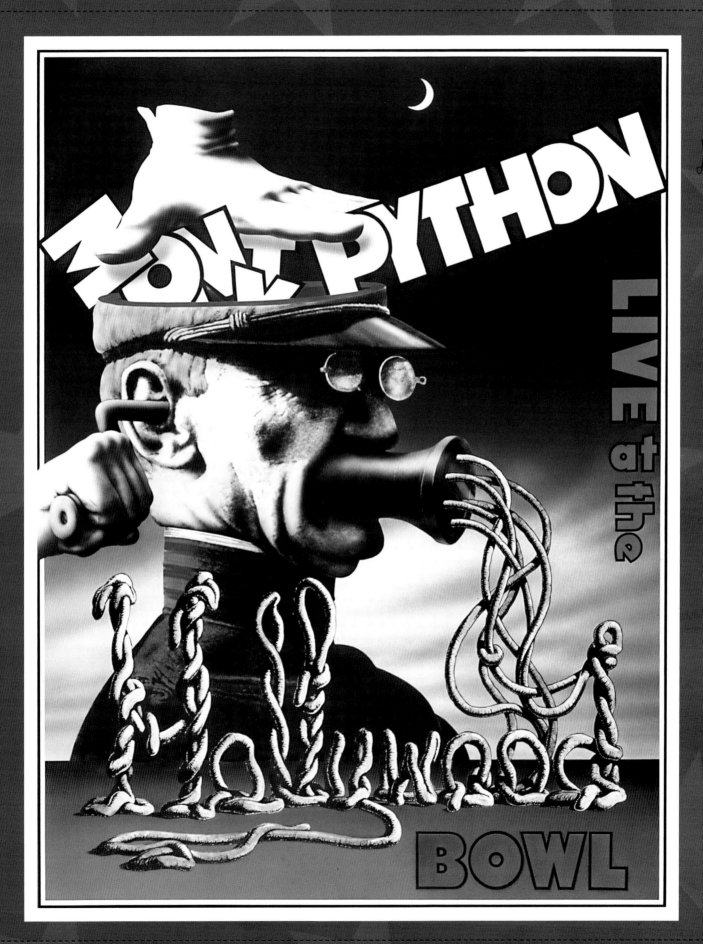

Piss Off

and filmed sketches from the largely unseen, German-shot *Fliegender Zirkkus* episodes. It was, to all intents and purposes, a rock concert. Backstage a huge hospitality set-up dispensed food and drink to a celebrity crowd, while out front the punters worked themselves up into a good-natured frenzy. "If the audience weren't on their feet cheering before we went out," says Terry G, "we wouldn't go out."

Michael introduced the show with the words, "Hello, good evening and welcome to the Ronald Reagan Memorial Bowl, here in the pretty little LA suburb of Hollywood." And it was like they had never been away. They waltzed through the old sketches, trying to get to the end of lines before the crowd shouted them out. The audience often joined in karaoke-style and laughed uproariously throughout – at one point, John had to admonish them for laughing at a straight line.

They had also freshened up the show with some new material. Most memorable perhaps was the rendition of "Sit on My Face", a cheeky oral sex-themed ditty sung to the melody of "Sing as We Go" by 1930s British singer Gracie Fields. It was sung by John, Graham and the two Terrys, all dressed in traditional waiter's outfits. As they turned to leave, they were revealed to be trouser- and underwear-free beneath their aprons and all presented a full moon to the audience.

Terry Jones also twice attempted to debut the operatic "Never Be Rude to an Arab" song, but was dragged offstage by a costumed frog before reaching the second verse of the ironically racist

number. His reprise in the second half of the show was similarly interrupted as he was blown up.

Particularly appreciated was "The Penultimate Supper", a Cleese–Chapman sketch only previously performed at *The Secret Policeman's Other Ball*, a 1976 benefit for Amnesty International, where John and Jonathan Lynn had taken the parts. Here, Eric played Michelangelo, who was being questioned by John as the Pope. His Holiness had some objections to some of the finer details of his painting…

POPE: I'm not happy with it.
MICHELANGELO: Oh, dear. It took hours.
POPE: No, not happy at all.
MICHELANGELO: Do the jellies worry you?
POPE: No.
MICHELANGELO: They add a bit of colour, don't they? Oh, I know, you don't like the kangaroo.
POPE: What kangaroo?
MICHELANGELO: I'll alter it, no sweat.
POPE: I never saw a kangaroo!
MICHELANGELO: It's right in the back. I'll paint it out, no problem. I'll make him into a disciple.
POPE: Aah.
MICHELANGELO: All right, now?
POPE: That's the problem.
MICHELANGELO: What is?
POPE: The disciples.
MICHELANGELO: Are they too Jewish? I made Judas the most Jewish.
POPE: No, no, it's just that there are 28 of them.
MICHELANGELO: Well, another one would hardly notice. So, I'll make the kangaroo into a disciple.

Other highlights included Carol Cleveland's out-of-time tap dancing as Neil Innes sang "I'm the Urban Spaceman", John excelling as he walked up and down the aisles hawking his albatross, and an extended "Travel Agent" ending in which Eric was chased around the Bowl and eventually interrupted the following sketch.

"I thought it was terrific. I'd never seen Eric perform better, he'd become a great sketch performer, and Michael was on form, and everybody was good."
John Cleese

Meanwhile, the Pythons were having a ball. They were relaxed and determined to have fun with each other and the audience. In the "Travel Agent" sketch, just as the audience anticipated Carol saying "…or would you like to come upstairs," she shocked them into silence with "…or would you like a blow job?" And when Michael, as was his wont, changed the last line of the "Parrot" sketch, a corpsing, befuddled John turned to the fans and asked them what the next line was. Of course, they duly supplied it. "There's 7,000 people out there and all we're doing is trying to make each other laugh!" was Terry G's comment.

The audience were so ecstatic and appreciative that the curtain calls lasted ten minutes, which was plenty of time for more silliness as the Pythons chased Carol across the stage and then reappeared being chased by her or everyone joined together for a can-can. Finally, when they had had enough, they signalled as much to the crowd by illuminating on the big screens the words "Piss Off".

Backstage they were meeting celebrities such as Joni Mitchell, Steve Martin (who later threw a party in their honour), Mick Jagger, John Belushi and Robin Williams. John met his second wife, Barbara Trentham, there (she would later say, "It was mild curiosity at first sight") and, according to Beatles biographer Keith Badman, John Lennon and Yoko Ono flew in to see the show and met up with George Harrison (Lennon was shot and killed just a couple of months later).

Under the starry Californian sky, with stadium-style production values and

organization, this was Python in another dimension. They were far away from West London backstreets, BBC studios, cold and wet Scottish landscapes or seemingly endless nights in city theatres, but it still worked. The Pythons enjoyed performing the material as much as, if not more than, they ever had and the audience savoured every word. It was the perfect way for the team to perform together for the last time.

THE BRUCES' PHILOSOPHERS SONG

Immanuel Kant was a real pissant
Who was very rarely stable

Heidegger, Heidegger was a boozy beggar
Who could think you under the table

David Hume could out-consume
Schopenhauer and Hegel

And Wittgenstein was a beery swine
Who was just as schloshed as Schlegel

There's nothing Nietzsche couldn't teach ya
'Bout the raising of the wrist
Socrates, himself, was permanently pissed

John Stuart Mill, of his own free will,
On half a pint of shandy was particularly ill

Plato, they say, could stick it away
Half a crate of whiskey every day

Aristotle, Aristotle was a bugger for the bottle
Hobbes was fond of his dram

And René Descartes was a drunken fart
"I drink, therefore I am"

Yes, Socrates, himself, is particularly missed
A lovely little thinker
But a bugger when he's pissed.

Monty Python **Live** at the Hollywood Bowl programme poster. These were sold at the show and enabled fans to join in and sing along...

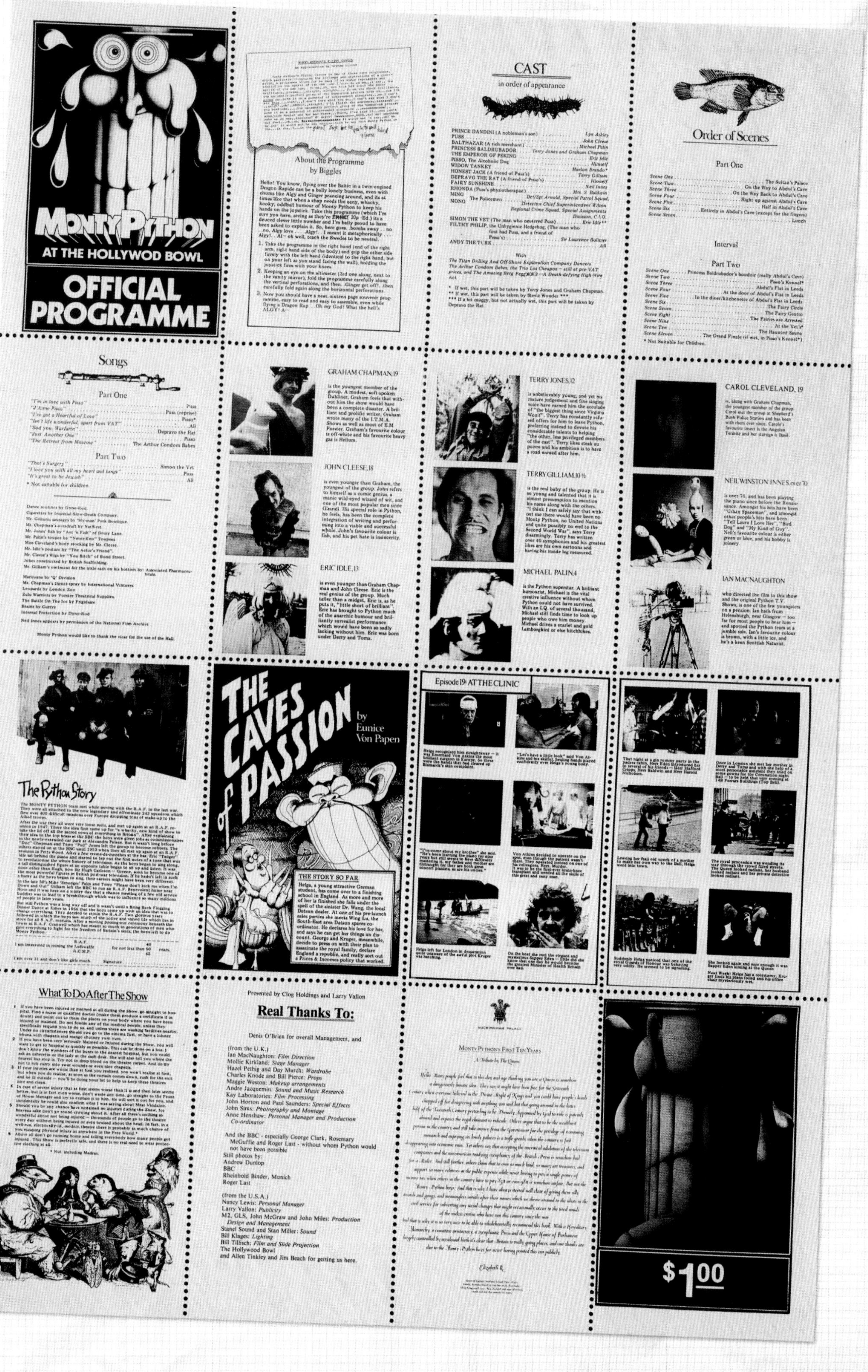

MONTY PYTHON

AT THE HOLLYWOOD BOWL

OFFICIAL PROGRAMME

About the Programme by Biggles

Hello! You know, flying over the Baltic in a twin-engined Dragon Rapide can be a bally lonely business, even with chums like Algy and Ginger prancing around, and its at times like that when a chap needs the zany, whacky, kooky, oddball humour of Monty Python to keep his hands on the joystick. Take this programme (which I'm sure you have, seeing as they're ~~FREE~~ 20p -Ed.) its a deuced clever little number and I'm bally proud to have been asked to explain it. So, here goes. .bombs away . . no . .no, Algy love . . . . Algy! . . I meant it metaphorically . . . . Algy! . . Al— oh well, teach the Swedes to be neutral.

1. Take the programme in the right hand (end of the right arm, right hand side of the body) and grip the other side firmly with the left hand (identical to the right hand, but on your left as you stand facing the wall), holding the joystick firm with your knees.
2. Keeping an eye on the altimeter (3rd one along, next to the vanity mirror), fold the programme carefully along the vertical perforations, and then. .Ginger get off!. .then carefully fold again along the horizontal perforations.
3. Now you should have a neat, sixteen page souvenir programme, easy to read and easy to assemble, even while flying a Dragon Rap. . .Oh my God! What the hell's ALGY! A—

CAST

in order of appearance

PRINCE DANDINI (A nobleman's son)	*Lyn Ashley*
PUSS	*John Cleese*
BALTHAZAR (A rich merchant)	*Michael Palin*
PRINCESS BALDRUBADOR	*Terry Jones and Graham Chapman*
THE EMPEROR OF PEKING	*Eric Idle*
PISSO, The Alcoholic Dog	*Himself*
WIDOW TANKEY	*Marlon Brando**
HONEST JACK (A friend of Puss's)	*Terry Gilliam*
DEPRAVO THE RAT (A friend of Pisso's)	*Himself*
FAIRY SUNSHINE	*Neil Innes*
RHONDA (Puss's physiotherapist)	*Mrs. S. Baldwin*
MING, MONG — The Policemen	*Det/Sgt Arnold, Special Patrol Squad, Detective Chief Superintendent Wilson Regional Crime Squad, Special Assignments Division, C.I.D.*
SIMON THE VET (The man who neutered Puss)	*Eric Idle***
FILTHY PHILIP, the Unhygienic Hedgehog, (The man who first had Puss, and a friend of Pisso's)	*Sir Laurence Bolivier*
ANDY THE TURK	*All*

With

The Titan Drilling And Off-Shore Exploration Company Dancers The Arthur Condom Babes, the Trio Los Cheapos — still at pre-VAT prices, and The Amazing Berg Fegg~~XX~~2 — A Death-defying High-Wire Act.

* If wet, this part will be taken by Terry Jones and Graham Chapman.
** If wet, this part will be taken by Stevie Wonder ***.
*** If a bit muggy, but not actually wet, this part will be taken by Depravo the Rat.

Order of Scenes

Part One

Scene One	The Sultan's Palace
Scene Two	On the Way to Abdul's Cave
Scene Three	On the Way Back to Abdul's Cave
Scene Four	Right up against Abdul's Cave
Scene Five	Half in Abdul's Cave
Scene Six	Entirely in Abdul's Cave (except for the fingers)
Scene Seven	Lunch

Interval

Part Two

Scene One	Princess Baldrubador's boudoir (really Abdul's Cave)
Scene Two	Pisso's Kennel*
Scene Three	Abdul's Flat in Leeds
Scene Four	At the door of Abdul's Flat in Leeds
Scene Five	In the diner/kitchenette of Abdul's Flat in Leeds
Scene Six	The Fairy Circle
Scene Seven	The Fairy Grotto
Scene Eight	The Fairies are Arrested
Scene Nine	At the Vet's*
Scene Ten	The Haunted Sauna
Scene Eleven	The Grand Finale (if wet, in Pisso's Kennel*)

* Not Suitable for Children.

Songs

Part One

"I'm in love with Pisso"	Puss
"J'Aime Pisso"	Puss (reprise)
"I've got a Heartful of Love"	Pisso*
"Isn't life wonderful, apart from VAT"	All
"Sod you, Warfarin"	Depravo the Rat
"Just Another One"	Pisso
"The Retreat from Moscow"	The Arthur Condom Babes

Part Two

"That's Surgery"	Simon the Vet
"I love you with all my heart and lungs"	Puss
"It's great to be Jewish"	All

* Not suitable for children.

Dance routines by Dyno-Rod.
Cigarettes by Imperial Slow-Death Company.
Mr. Gilliam's sausages by 'My-man' Pork Boutique.
Mr. Chapman's overdraft by NatWest.
Mr. Jones' fish by "Art 'n Fish" of Drury Lane.
Mr. Palin's toupee by "Never-Kno" Toupees
Miss Cleveland's body stocking by Mr. Cleese.
Mr. Idle's posture by "The Actor's Friend".
Mr. Cleese's Wigs by "You Bitch" of Bond Street.
Jokes constructed by British Scaffolding.
Mr. Gilliam's ointment for the little rash on his bottom by: Associated Pharmaceuticals.
Marijuana by 'Q' Division
Mr. Chapman's throat-spray by International Vintners.
Leopards by London Zoo
Zulu Warriors by Vorster Theatrical Supplies.
The Battle On The Ice by Frigidaire
Brains by Currys
Internal Protection by Dyno-Rod

Neil Innes appears by permission of the National Film Archive

Monty Python would like to thank the vicar for the use of the Hall.

GRAHAM CHAPMAN, 19

is the youngest member of the group. A modest, soft-spoken Dubliner, Graham feels that without him the show would have been a complete disaster. A brilliant and prolific writer, Graham wrote many of the I.T.M.A. Shows as well as most of E.M. Forster. Graham's favourite colour is off-white and his favourite heavy gas is Helium.

JOHN CLEESE, 18

is even younger than Graham, the youngest of the group. John refers to himself as a comic genius, a manic wild-eyed wizard of wit, and one of the most popular men since Ghandi. His special role in Python, he feels, has been the complete integration of writing and performing into a viable and successful whole. John's favourite colour is fish, and his pet hate is insincerity.

ERIC IDLE, 13

is even younger than Graham Chapman and John Cleese. Eric is the real genius of the group. Much taller than a midget, Eric is, as he puts it, "little short of brilliant". Eric has brought to Python much of the anarchic humour and brilliantly surrealist performance which would have been so sadly lacking without him. Eric was born under Derry and Toms.

TERRY JONES, 12

is unbelievably young, and yet his mature judgement and fine singing voice have earned him the accolade of "the biggest thing since Virginia Woolf". Terry has constantly refused offers for him to leave Python, preferring instead to devote his considerable talents to helping "the other, less privileged members of the cast". Terry likes steak au poivre and his ambition is to have a road named after him.

TERRY GILLIAM, 10½

is the real baby of the group. He is so young and talented that it is almost presumption to mention his name along with the others. "I think I can safely say that without me there would have been no Monty Python, no United Nations and quite possibly no end to the Second World War", says Terry disarmingly. Terry has written over 40 symphonies and his greatest likes are his own cartoons and having his inside leg measured.

MICHAEL PALIN, 4

is the Python superstar. A brilliant humourist, Michael is the vital creative influence without whom Python could not have survived. With an I.Q. of several thousand, Michael still finds time to look up people who owe him money. Michael drives a scarlet and gold Lamborghini or else hitchhikes.

CAROL CLEVELAND, 19

is, along with Graham Chapman, the youngest member of the group. Carol met the group at Shepherd's Bush Police Station and has been with them ever since. Carole's favourite insect is the Angolan Termite and her starsign is Basil.

NEIL WINSTON INNES, over 70

is over 70, and has been playing the piano since before the Renaissance. Amongst his hits have been "Urban Spaceman", and amongst other people's hits have been "Tell Laura I Love Her", "Bird Dog" and "My Kind of Guy". Neil's favourite colour is either green or blue, and his hobby is joinery.

IAN MACNAUGHTON

who directed the film in this show and the original Python T.V. Shows, is one of the few youngsters on a pension. Ian hails from Helensburgh, near Glasgow — too far for most people to hear him — and spotted the Python team at a jumble sale. Ian's favourite colour is brown, with a little ice, and he's a keen Scottish Naturist.

The Python Story

The MONTY PYTHON team met while serving with the R.A.F. in the last war. They were all attached to the now legendary and effeminate 243 squadron which flew over 400 difficult missions over Europe dropping tons of make-up to the Allied troops.

After the war they all wore very loose suits, and met up again at an R.A.F. reunion in 1947. There the idea first came up for "a whacky, new kind of show to take the lid off all the sacred cows of everything in Britain". After explaining their idea to the top brass at the BBC the boys were given jobs as commissionaires in the newly-extended car park at Alexandra Palace. But it wasn't long before "Doc" Chapman and Terry "Pud" Jones left the group to become robbers. The others stayed on at the BBC until 1953 when they all met up again at an R.A.F. reunion in Petts Wood. After a few creme-de-menthes at the bar, Eric "Tadger" Idle sat behind the piano and started to tap out the first notes of a tune that was to revolutionise the whole history of television. As the boys began to sing along, a tall distinguished figure at an opposite table began to sit up and listen. It was none other than Hugh, now Sir Hugh Carleton — Greene, soon to become one of the most powerful figures in British post-war television. If he hadn't left in such a hurry as the boys began to sing, their careers might have been very different.

In the late 50's Mike 'Smudger' Palin and Terry "Please don't kick me when I'm Down and Out" Gilliam left the BBC to run an R.A.F. Benevolent home near Hove and it was here on a wintry day that a chance meeting of a few old service buddies was to lead to a breakthrough which was to influence so many millions of people in later years.

But still Python was a long way off and it wasn't until a Bring Back Flogging Dinner Dance at Esher in 1966 that the boys came up with an idea that was to change everything. They decided to rejoin the R.A.F. Two glorious years followed in which the boys saw much of the active and varied life which lies in store for all R.A.F. recruits. After a moving passing-out ceremony beneath the tower at R.A.F. Cranwell which has meant so much to generations of men who gave everything to fight for the freedom of Britain's skies, the boys left to do Monty Python.

I am interested in joining the R.A.F. / Luftwaffe / R.C.M.P. for not less than 40 / 50 / 65 years.

I am over 21 and don't like girls much. Signature . . . .

THE CAVES OF PASSION

by Eunice Von Papen

THE STORY SO FAR

Helga, a young attractive German student, has come over to a finishing school in England. As more and more of her is finished she falls under the spell of the sinister Dr. Wang, the local Datsun dealer. At one of his pre-launch sales parties she meets Wing Lu, the South-East area Datsun spares co-ordinator. He declares his love for her, and says he can get her things on discount. George and Kruger, meanwhile, decide to press on with their plan to assassinate the royal family, declare England a republic, and really sort out a Prices & Incomes policy that worked.

Episode 19: AT THE CLINIC

Helga recognised him straightaway — it was Emerhard Von Atkins the most brilliant surgeon in Europe. So these were the hands that had cleared up Bismarck's skin complaint.

"Let's have a little look" said Von Atkins and his skilful, healing hands played confidently over Helga's young body.

"I've come about my brother" she said. "He's been learning the piano for nine years but still seems to have difficulty mastering it, my father and mother are distraught for they are both great concert pianists, as are his uncles."

Von Atkins decided to operate on the spot, even though the patient wasn't there. They operated instead on one of his colleagues, Herr. Murder. It was to be the first-ever brain-knee transplant and needed all the skills of this great and zany man.

Helga left for London in desperation quite unaware of the awful plot Kruger was hatching.

On the boat she met the elegant and mysterious Sapper Eden — little did she know that one day he would become the greatest Minister of Health Britain ever had.

That night at a gin rummy party in the padres cabin, Herr Eden introduced her to several of his friends — Herr Stafford Cripps, Herr Baldwin and Herr Harold Nicholson.

Once in London she met her mother in Derry and Toms and with the help of a most personable assistant they tried on some gowns for the Coronation night Ball — to be held that very evening at 14B Ferrars Buildings (Top Bell).

Leaving her frail old wreck of a mother to make her own way to the Ball, Helga went into town.

The royal procession was wending its way through the crowd filled streets. The Queen looked radiant, her husband looked radiant and her private detective looked radiant.

Suddenly Helga noticed that one of the royal Guards of Honour was behaving very oddly. He seemed to be signalling.

She looked again and sure enough it was Sapper Eden aiming at the Queen.

Next Week: Helga has a colostomy, Kruger finds his plans foiled and his office chair mysteriously wet.

What To Do After The Show

1. If you have been injured or maimed at all during the Show, go straight to hospital. Find a nurse or qualified doctor (make them produce a certificate if in doubt) and point out to them the places on your body where you have been injured or maimed. Do not fondle any of the medical people, unless they specifically request you to do so, and unless there are washing facilities nearby. Under no circumstances should you go to the cinema first, or have a lobster bhuna with chapatis and mango chutney yum yum.
2. If you have been very seriously Maimed or Injured during the Show, you will want to get to hospital as quickly as possible. This can be done on a bus. I don't know the numbers of the buses to the nearest hospital, but you could ask an usherette or the lady at the cash desk. She will also tell you where the nearest bus stop is. Try not to drop blood on the theatre carpet. And do try not to rub curry into your wounds or even nice chapatis.
3. If your injuries are worse than at first you realised, you won't realise at first, but when you do realise, as soon as the curtain comes down, rush for the exit and be ill outside — you'll be doing your bit to help us keep these theatres nice and clean.
4. In case of severe injury that at first seems worse than it is and then later seems better, but is in fact even worse, don't waste any time, go straight to the Front of House Manager and try to explain it to him. He will sort it out for you, and incidentally he could also confirm what I was saying about Meat Vindaloo.
5. Should you by any chance have sustained no injuries during the Show, for heavens sake don't go round crowing about it. After all there's nothing so wonderful about not being injured — thousands of people go to the theatre every day without being injured or even bruised about the head. In fact, in a well-run, electrically-lit, modern theatre there is probably as much chance of you escaping physical injury as anywhere in the Free World.*
6. Above all don't go running home and telling everybody how many people got injured. This Show is perfectly safe, and there is no real need to wear protective clothing at all.

* Not including Madras.

Presented by Clog Holdings and Larry Vallon

Real Thanks To:

Denis O'Brien for overall Management, and

(from the U.K.)
Ian MacNaughton: *Film Direction*
Mollie Kirkland: *Stage Manager*
Hazel Pethig and Day Murch: *Wardrobe*
Charles Knode and Bill Pierce: *Props*
Maggie Weston: *Makeup arrangements*
Andre Jacquemin: *Sound and Music Research*
Kay Laboratories: *Film Processing*
John Horton and Paul Saunders: *Special Effects*
John Sims: *Photography and Montage*
Anne Henshaw: *Personal Manager and Production Co-ordinator*

And the BBC - especially George Clark, Rosemary McGuffie and Roger Last - without whom Python would not have been possible
Still photos by:
Andrew Dunlop
BBC
Rheinhold Binder, Munich
Roger Last

(from the U.S.A.)
Nancy Lewis: *Personal Manager*
Larry Vallon: *Publicity*
M2, GLS, John McGraw and John Miles: *Production Design and Management*
Stanel Sound and Stan Miller: *Sound*
Bill Klages: *Lighting*
Bill Tillisch: *Film and Slide Projection*
The Hollywood Bowl
and Allen Tinkley and Jim Beach for getting us here.

BUCKINGHAM PALACE

Monty Python's First Ten Years

A Tribute by The Queen

Hello. Many people feel that in this day and age thinking you are a Queen is somehow a dangerously lunatic idea. They say it might have been fine for the Sixteenth Century when everyone believed in the Divine Right of Kings and you could have people's heads chopped off for disagreeing with anything you said but that going around in the latter half of the Twentieth Century pretending to be Divinely Appointed by God to rule is patently absurd and exposes the regal claimant to ridicule. Others argue that to be the wealthiest person in the country and still take money from the Government for the privilege of remaining monarch and enjoying six lovely palaces is a trifle greedy when the country is fast disappearing into economic ruin. Yet others say that accepting the uncritical adulation of the television companies and the unceasing toadying sycophancy of the British Press is somehow bad for a Ruler. And still further, others claim that to own so much land, so many art treasures, and support so many relatives at the public expense while never having to pay a single penny of income tax when others in the country have to pay 83% or even 98% is somehow unfair. But not the Monty Python boys. And that is why I have always steered well clear of giving them silly awards and gongs, and meaningless initials after their names which we throw around to the idiots in the civil service for subverting any social changes that might occasionally occur to the tired minds of the witless cretins who have run this country since the war.

And that is why it is so very nice to be able to wholeheartedly recommend this book. With a Hereditary Monarchy, a comatose aristocracy, a sycophantic Press and the Upper House of Parliament largely controlled by accidental birth it's clear that Britain is really going places, and our thanks are due to the Monty Python boys for never having pointed this out publicly.

Elizabeth R

$1.00

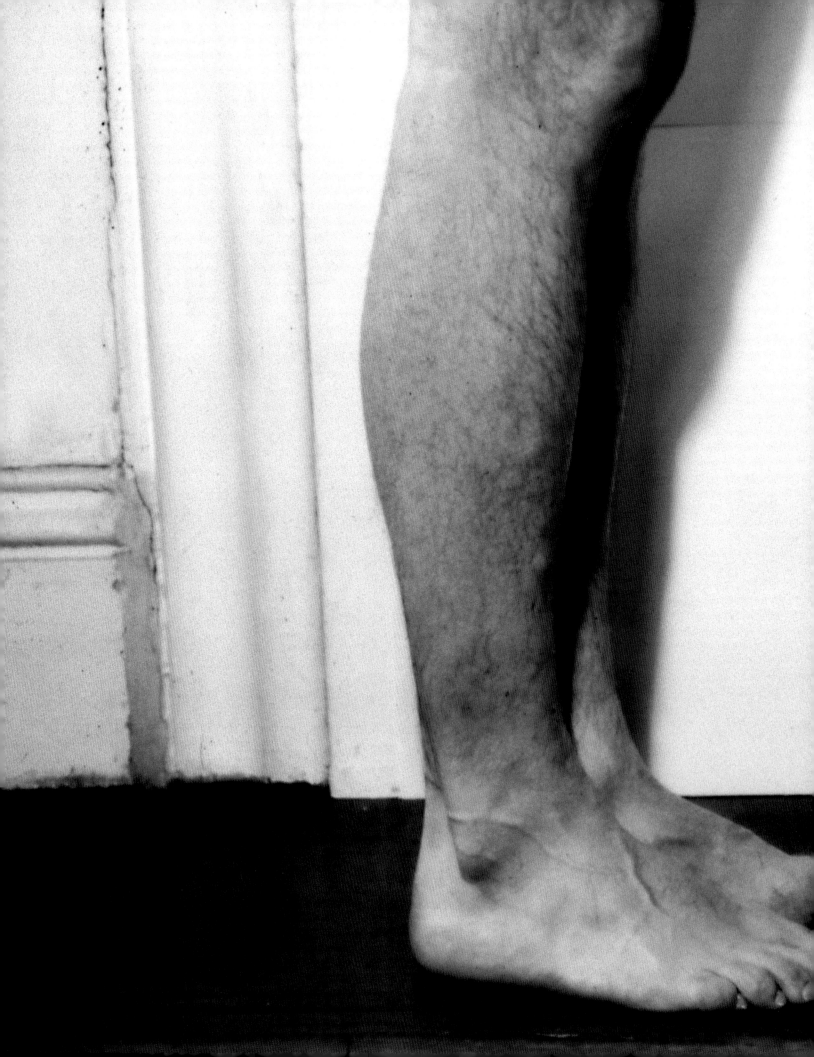

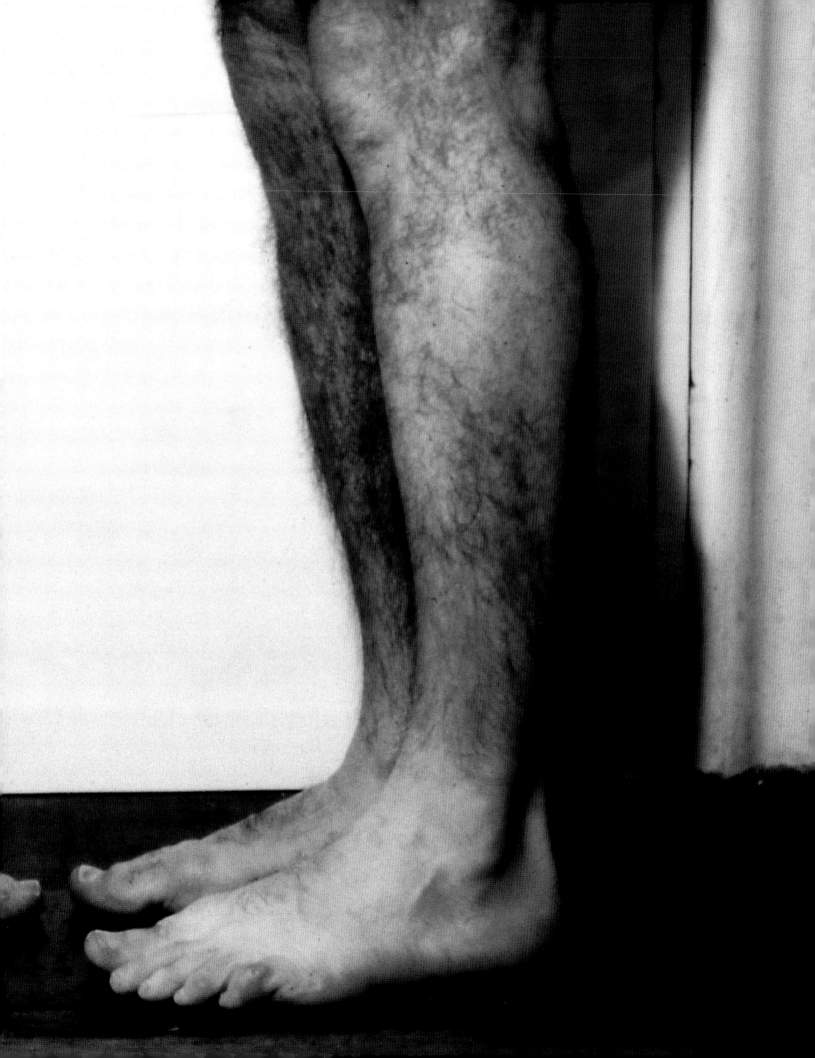

The Inbetween Years

The BBC has religiously celebrated the ten-year anniversaries of *Flying Circus*. As early as 1979, the tenth anniversary year, it produced a documentary on the team which was shot in Tunisia during the filming of *Life of Brian*. On this occasion, Michael Palin's It's Man was even featured as the cover picture on the BBC's listings magazine, *Radio Times*.

Above: *Radio Times*, the BBC's TV listings magazine celebrates the 10th anniversary of Monty Python with the It's Man appearing on the front cover.

In 1989, the 20th anniversary was marked by appearances by various Pythons, an exhibition at the Museum of Broadcasting in New York, the publication by Methuen of two volumes of the *Flying Circus* scripts and *Parrot Sketch Not Included*, a 90-minute "Best of Flying Circus" feature presented by Steve Martin. *The Pythons Autobiography* notes a sequence was

Above: Joined by comedian Eddie Izzard, members of *Monty Python's Flying Circus* took to BBC2 to celebrate the programme's 30th anniversary in 1999.

shot for this in which the Pythons dressed as school boys, asked Martin questions and wrote down his answers. This was cut from the show as the group regarded it as embarrassing and unfunny. Instead, the programme contained a very brief finale in which Steve Martin reveals all the Pythons crammed into a wardrobe.

These few seconds of footage

were the last time they appeared together. Graham, who had been suffering from throat cancer, died on the eve of the anniversary.

The Pythons, some of whom were at his bedside as he died, were deeply shocked by his passing. The memorial service was held at St Graham's old hospital college, St Bartholomew's, where he was given a send-off that included Neil Innes singing 'How Sweet to be an Idiot', Eric leading a rendition of 'Always Look on the Bright Side of Life' and John's now famous eulogy.

"HE HAS CEASED TO BE, BEREFT OF LIFE, HE RESTS IN PEACE, HE HAS KICKED THE BUCKET, HOPPED THE TWIG, BIT THE DUST, SNUFFED IT, BREATHED HIS LAST, AND GONE TO MEET THE GREAT HEAD OF LIGHT ENTERTAINMENT IN THE SKY, AND I GUESS THAT WE'RE ALL THINKING HOW SAD IT IS THAT A MAN OF SUCH TALENT, SUCH CAPABILITY AND KINDNESS, OF SUCH INTELLIGENCE, SHOULD NOW BE SO SUDDENLY SPIRITED AWAY AT THE AGE OF ONLY 48, BEFORE HE'D ACHIEVED MANY OF THE THINGS OF WHICH HE WAS

CAPABLE, AND BEFORE HE'D HAD ENOUGH FUN. WELL, I FEEL THAT I SHOULD SAY, "NONSENSE. GOOD RIDDANCE TO HIM, THE FREELOADING BASTARD! I HOPE HE FRIES." AND THE REASON I THINK I SHOULD SAY THIS IS HE WOULD NEVER FORGIVE ME IF I DIDN'T, IF I THREW AWAY THIS OPPORTUNITY TO SHOCK YOU ALL ON HIS BEHALF. ANYTHING FOR HIM BUT MINDLESS GOOD TASTE." OPENING OF JOHN'S EULOGY AT GRAHAM CHAPMAN'S MEMORIAL SERVICE

Above: In 1999 Michael Palin revisited Teddington Lock, home of the fish-slapping dance for *Pythonland*.

Above: A rare reunion for the Pythons saw them perform a short Gumbys routine for the 1999 special.

Above: The (apparently) staged joke where Graham Chapman's remains were desecrated on stage in the name of comedy, at the US Comedy Arts Festival in Aspen, Colorado, in 1998.

Whispers and rumours abounded before the 30th anniversary after the surviving Pythons had finally appeared together the previous year. In Aspen, Colorado, in 1998, as part of the US Comedy Arts Festival, Robert Klein hosted a fun and frank interview in front of a small theatre audience. The biggest laugh of the evening was a staged joke in which Terry G kicks over the urn purporting to contain Graham's ashes.

"WE TRIED TO DO SOMETHING THAT WAS SO UNPREDICTABLE THAT IT HAD NO SHAPE AND YOU COULD NEVER SAY WHAT THE KIND OF HUMOUR WAS. AND I THINK THE FACT THAT 'PYTHONESQUE' IS NOW A WORD IN THE OXFORD ENGLISH DICTIONARY SHOWS THE EXTENT TO WHICH WE FAILED." TERRY JONES, US COMEDY ARTS FESTIVAL, 1998

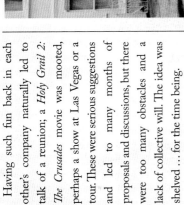

Above: John Cleese back in announcer mode for the BBC's 30th anniversary extravaganza.

Below: Eric Idle kept the Python flame alive through the years after Hollywood Bowl.

Having such fun back in each other's company naturally led to talk of a reunion; a *Holy Grail 2: The Crusades* movie was mooted, perhaps a show at Las Vegas or a tour. These were serious suggestions and led to many months of proposals and discussions, but there were too many obstacles and a lack of collective will. The idea was shelved ... for the time being.

For the 30th anniversary, the BBC devoted a whole evening to Python Night. The entertainment included *It's ... the Monty Python Story*, an Eddie Izzard-hosted documentary complete with celebrity tributes; *Pythonland*, in which Michael Palin returned to the original locations of some of the filmed sketches; *From Spam to Sperm: Monty Python's Greatest Hits* with Meat Loaf recounting the stories behind various Python musical highlights; and a much-heralded Peter Sissons interview with all the remaining Pythons, which terminated after they had each said, "Good evening."

In 2009, the end of the fourth decade of Monty Python was commemorated with a six-part documentary, *Monty Python: Almost the Truth (The Lawyers Cut)*, and an official 40th anniversary reunion took place in New York City on October 22, 2009, where the team received a Special Award from the British Academy of Film and Television Arts (BAFTA). Although they appeared on a panel together, it still seemed unlikely they would ever perform as a group again.

Eric Idle and "Queen Elizabeth II" (or, rather, a look-alike hired by the Pythons), pictured on a mock Silver Jubilee postcard from 1977.

喜劇電影週

HERE COMES MONTY PYTHON

23-30 • 9 • 1988

Presented by 主辦機構   The British Council 英國文化協會   香港藝術中心 HONG KONG ARTS CENTRE   藝穗會 Fringe Club

CRACKPOT: (cont'd...)

Lower class - I can't touch it. There's no return on it, you see - I'd like to, we've got plans for expanding the business - but this is only a family religion, you see. My mother, God Bless her who was a free-lance font in Epping, was quite keen that we should not go public. Her dying words were "Look out for the poor". Then again (TAPPING THE BOOK) there's the texts against poverty.

"Sell all you have an go into nickel". And of course the one that puts the kybosh on it - this is the real chopper - "It is as easy for a poor man to enter heaven as for a spaniel to go through finest quality Fisher and Ludlow ¼" tensile stainless steel tubing." There's no way round that one you see - it's what we in religion call an excluding clause.

INT:

I though it was "rich man, camel and needle's eye".

"Crackpot Religions." This is a cut section from the sketch in Series Two.

- 32 -

CRACKPOT:
The old camel and needle
story yeah - well the camel
and needle story was a bit
of slander put around by some
Jewish fellers who wanted to
make a quick buck by scaring
the market. And of course it
worked. They got quite a business
out of it.

INT:
Do you have any difficulty
converting people?

CRACKPOT:
Oh no - we have ways of making
them join.

CAPTION:

CUT TO: EXCEEDINGLY THICK, HUGE
 TOUGH, SUPER CAPTION:

   "The Bishop of Dulwich".

(V/O) Norman there does a lot
of converting - a lot of
caring about people - a lot of
protection, that sort of thing.
And there's his mate - Bruce
Beer.

AN ENORMOUS AUSTRALIAN BOOZER.
                SUPER CAPTION:

"The Archbishop of Australia".

Brucie has personally converted/

[~~~~~~ MR 3/14 ~~~] COURT SKETCH

A COURTROOM.
VARIOUS DUMMIES IN THE JURY BOX (CAROL'S
TWO SINGING DUMMIES PLUS THE BRUCES POSSIBLY).

ERIC IN THE DOCK. TERRY THE JUDGE. MIKE, ONE
COUNSEL. NEIL, CLERK OF COURT. CAROL THE TYPIST.
TERRY GILLIAM THE JURY.

JUDGE: Smith   Stand [charged with] here
Michael Norman ~~Randall~~ you ~~have been found~~
                          Arthur Edward Hopcraft,
~~guilty~~ of the murder of ~~the~~ Right Reverend
Brian Graham Whittaker, Malcolm Kenelm Bennett,
Arthur Claud Webster, Bishop of Leicester,
Peter Sebastopol Lewis, Rita Anne Merkelis, Viscount
Charles Patrick Trumpington Bishop of
Mike
Lynsey de Paul, Fräulein Ilse   Yallop, Lieutenant-General Sir
~~Birmingham~~, Ronald ~~Victor~~ Harmsworth, ~~Bishop of~~
Richard Stanley-Booth, and Stanley Booth, Cynthia
~~Leeds~~, Prebendary Charles MacIntyre Potter,
Jane Stanley-Booth, Richard Edward Stanley-Booth, Vanessa
~~Moderator of the Church of Scotland~~, Reverend
'Snakehips'   Stanley-Booth and Master Paul Stanley-Booth,
the Nigel ~~Sinclair~~ Robinson, Reverend John Claud

Motson, Father Kevin Joyce O'Malley, ~~Dean Robert~~

~~William Palmer~~, Monsignor Jean-Paul Reynard,

Padre Robert Henry Noonan, Rabbis Edwin and Carey
                                    Gingold
Makepeace ~~Goodgold~~, Pope ~~Pius~~ Mario Vercotti,
Divisional Fire Officer
~~Pastor~~ Karl-Heinz Biolek, Archbishop Stavros
            Abplanalp
Nicolas ~~Parsonas~~, His Most Holy and In~~di~~visible
                          Bombardier
Oneness Hwang Ky Sung and ~~Raj~~ Arthur Buddha,
                    morning of the
on or about the [third] Sunday in Epiphany.

Have you anything to say before this court

considers your case ~~and passes sentence upon you~~?

SMITH
~~RANDALL~~:
Yes sir, I'm very sorry. It was a very bad
            do, and
thing to ~~have done~~ and ~~I'm really very~~ ashamed
~~of myself.~~ I can only say it won't happen
again. ~~I really feel~~

for RANDALL
read SMITH throughout

JUDGE: Mr Smith!
~~Oh shut up~~! How do you plead

RANDALL HOLDS TWO FINGERS UP AND DEMONSTRATES
TO COURT A LA CHARADES

RANDALL: Well I did it.
JUDGE   You did it
RANDALL   Yes.
ALL: (disappointed) Oh.

RANDALL: But I know how much you've all been looking
             forward to this so I'm going to plead Not Guilty

ALL   Oh Good.

JUDGE: Thank you Mr Smith. ~~And that the change~~   Counsel for the prosecution
             ~~Now that the change has been set~~.

TYPIST: Sorry your honour. How ~~do you~~ do you...

JUDGE: What ~~do you want~~? ...?

TYPIST: How do you spell that. ~~this~~ S.M.I ~~Sto~~ then
             I go a bit wrong.

JUDGE   what Smith??

TYPIST   Yes your honour.

JUDGE   T.H !

TYPIST   Oh of course thank you

JUDGE   Right. ~~the~~ Counsel for the prosecution

~~the~~ P.C. Yes m' lud.

TYPIST   Sorry.

JUDGE   ~~Well?~~ What is it

TYPIST   Charged with ~~but~~ murder is it?

JUDGE   I beg your pardon.?

TYPIST   ~~his murder is it?~~ What did you say right after Smith... stand here charged with

JUDGE   Is that as far as you've got

TYPIST   Er.

JUDGE   Oh just get down what you can. Counsel for the prosecution

PC   Yes m'lord.

JUDGE   ... where is counsel for the defence.

PC   He's not here yet m'lord. He said could we start without him

DC (entering)   Sorry I'm late m'lord I couldn't find a hostel car park. Don't bother to recap m'lord ~~his~~ I'll pick it up as I go along. ~~Now you are~~

....

No, that's not it - carry on.

With respect, sir, I shall seek to prove that the accused
being in the employ of the British Army, and using expensive British
army equipment - to wit whit: one pair of boots, value
£3xixx £3.7s, one helmet, value £2, and one pair of gaiters
value £68.10s, chose, instead, to use his own teeth to
bite through ...

JUDGE: £68.10s for a pair of gaiters ?

PROS: They were special gaiters, sir.

JUDGE: Special gaiters ?

PROS: Yes...they were made in France. To bite, with deliberate and
           malicious intent...

JUDGE: What was special about them ?

PROS: (DISMISSIVELY) Oh...they were made of special fabric - the buckles
           were made of Empire silver instead of brass ... But his
           way

JUDGE: Why was he wearing special gaiters ?

PROS: They were a presentation pair, from the Regiment, sir.
           But his way, though officers and men alike, with cold
           and premeditated intent to ....

JUDGE: Why did they present him with a
           special pair of gaiters?

PROS: Sir I hardly feel it is relevant
           to the case..whether his gaiters
           were presented or not.

JUDGE: I think the court will be able to
           judge that for themselves. Why
           did the Regiment present the accused
           with a special pair of gaiters.

PROS: (STIFLING HIS IMPATIENCE)...He...used
           to do things for them. This total
           values. disregard
           for the lives
           of others...
           this...

CAMS	ACTION	SOUND

G.S.:
The idea is that Evans missed
the boat and his daughter stowed away
on the sledge, and then both Scott
and Oates fall in love with her,
so after they've beaten Amundesen,
the Russian, to the pole, in that
famous scene when Oates leaves
the tent, what really happens is
that he's gone to the bathroom,
and Scott's so jealous of him
that while he's away, Scott moves
the tent. Oates comes back and is
he mad?

(CUT TO CC AND TL STANDING ON BEACH)

T.L:
Well I see Oates as a pretty
wiv-it sort of geezer one day
'is mate Scott says 'Hey Oatsie'
'Let's ease down to the south pole
like, so Oatsie thinks it's a bit
of a giggle, why not, can't be bad,
so they nick the gear, they only
breeze down the pole don' they, then
they both get a bit keen on this
Evans bint, there you go, Oatsie pulls
her at the pole, bit of the full
frontal, Scottie gets narked, cuts
him out the deal, during breaks on
the set I do unpublicised work for

/Contd...

CAMS	ACTION	SOUND

T.L.(CONTD.)
charity, design power stations,
I'm writing a trilogy of novels
about Pericles but I'd really
like to settle down and paint,
away from artificial values,
can't be bad and that. There
you go.

(MAN RUNS IN)

MAN:
Mr. Lemming could we have you on
the set please.

(CUT TO GS AND CC STANDING IN FRONT
OF TENT)

G.S.:
We've decided this afternoon to shoot
the scene where Scott gets off the
boat on to the ice floe and he
sees the lion ahd he fights it and
kills it and the blood goes psssssssghhhh
(INDICATING in slow motion.

C.C.:
But there aren't any lions in the
Antartic

G.S.: What?

C.C.:There aren't any lions in the
Antarctic

GS. You're right. There are no lions
in the Antarctic. That's ridiculous;
whoever heard ...of a lion in the
Antarctic. Right(SHOUTS) Lose the lion.

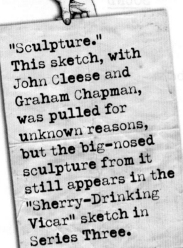

ACTION   SOUND

R:
(NOW FINDING HIMSELF BY THE STATUE
AND TEMPTED TO SHORTEN THE NOSE)
Well ....

S:
Oh ho ho!   Now we shall see.

Get the expert in eh?

Go on Mayor Rodin, it's all yours

now.   I'm just watching.   I've

only sculpted Brian Phelps and

King Farouk's nephew and Mrs Sidney

Green and Helen Shapiro's cousin

and unimportant people like that

so what would I know.   Huh.

R:
Well...

S:
Oh go on go on.   This should be

fascinating.

(IN ONE SWIFT CLEAN MOVEMENT
R KNOCKS OFF THE RIGHT LENGTH
OF NOSE AND STANDS BACK NERVOUSLY,
THEN LOOKING SATISFIED)

S:
(SARKY STILL)   Oh that's much

better.   Oh yes that makes all

the difference doesn't it?

(THEN NOTICING THAT IT REALLY HAS)

.... it is better isn't it?

ACTION   SOUND

R:
Well I may not know much about art

but I know what I'm like.

S:
(ADMIRING THE STATUE)

That really is very good.

R:
Thank you.

S:
Here... you do me.   Gavin!

(S GOES AND SITS DOWN IN THE
MODELS CHAIR.   GAVIN PUSHES A BLOCK
OF MARBLE IN FRONT OF R.)

S:
Ready?

R:
No really I couldn't.

S:
Come on, you have nothing to lose

but your chain.

R:
I don't know how to start.

S:
It's quite simple.   Just knock

away the bits that don't look like me.

(SHERRIFF WALKS THROUGH DOOR AND
CROSSES ROOM AS R STARTS TENTATIVELY)

SHERIFF:
Howdy folks. Mr. Mayor.

Everything peaceable round here?

R:
Yes thank you Sheriff.

(HE EXITS. S IS LOOKING AFTER
HIM, PUZZLED)

R:
Face the front please.

(S. DOES SO.   WE CLOSE IN
ON HIM AS BUZZING STARTS.
HE LOOKS AROUND AND THEN
MOVES HIS HEAD)

R:
Don't move.

S:
Sorry....

(BUZZING STOPS. CLOSE UP OF BEE
ON SCULPTOR'S HEAD.   THEN FROM
A WIDER SHOT WE SEE A BEEKEEPER
LOOKING ROUND THE DOOR CARRYING
A HUGE NET.   HIS EYES HAVE
ALIGHTED ON THE BEE.   AT THIS
MOMENT ANOTHER BEE KEEPER ALSO
WITH A HUGE NET APPEARS AT THE DOOR
OPPOSITE.   THE BEEKEEPERS SEE
EACH OTHER REGISTER INTENSE
RIVALRY RUSH TO S AND BRING DOWN
THE NETS OVER S'S HEAD.
WILD BUZZING CAN BE HEARD.)

B1:
It's my bee.

B2:
It isn't.

B1:
It is.

B2:
It is not it's mine.

B1:
All right if it's your bee

describe it.

B2:
It's sort of furry with orange

and brown stripes round its

middle and it makes honey.

B1:
(MIMING ANTENNAE BUT NOT CLEOPATRA)

Does it have long things like this.

B2:
Yes it does.

B1:
Does it have eight legs.

B2:
No it has six and it's name is

Darryl.

B1:
It is not it's name is Mick.

ONE DOWN
FIVE TO GO

JULY 1-5, 1[...]
THE O2

MONTY PYTHON
LIVE (mostly)

5, 18-20 2014
ONDON

Monty Python Live
(mostly) - One Down
Five to Go poster from
the reunion shows at
The 02 in London, 2014.

When the reunion show finally came, it was fitting that Eric was responsible for producing the monumental event. He had continued to fly the Python flag with stage tours such as *Eric Idle Exploits Monty Python* (2000), the Tony Award-winning musical *Spamalot* (2005), which, as he admitted, "lovingly ripped off" *Holy Grail*, a Life of Brian-inspired oratorio entitled *He's Not the Messiah...* (2007) and a sparkling rendition of "Always Look on the Bright Side of Life" at the 2012 Olympics closing ceremony.

But Monty Python was always about the collective and, in November 2013, the five got together to announce their reunion. In July 2014, they performed *Monty Python Live (Mostly) – One Down Five to Go* at London's largest indoor venue, the 16,000-seater 02 Arena in London. It was their biggest ever show, with all ten shows selling out.

For seven years, the Pythons had been fighting a court case over *Spamalot* royalties and the legal bills had become astronomical. Jim Beach, manager of the pop group Queen and an old friend of the Pythons came up with a simple solution – play one night at London's 02 and they could pay off the whole debt. If the group were ever going to reform, this was surely the occasion – one last triumphant bow in front of fans who had stayed loyal through the years; "a pre-posthumous memorial service" as Terry Gilliam called it. The decision to go ahead was spontaneous and unanimous.

Part of the appeal was that, much like the Hollywood Bowl, it was an opportunity to do Python in a different setting. Their 02 show would be a full-on musical extravaganza with chorus singers, massed dancers, full use of the gigantic screens, enabling Graham and Terry G's animations to feature prominently, and, of course, everyone's favourite sketches. And, not only would the five Pythons be back, so too would Carol Cleveland and other long-time Python friends and collaborators, including costume designer Hazel Pethig and soundman Andre Jacqueman

When tickets went on sale the response was phenomenal. The proposed one-night show sold out in 43.5 seconds, so they decided to do four more. Those sold out within an hour. Eventually, they settled on ten shows, all in July 2014, during which they would play to over 150,000 people.

The Pythons realized they were no longer as sprightly as their 1970s selves. Although young at heart, a large stage, more than a dozen costume changes and some physical drama was going to tax their energy and ageing limbs. To counter these obstacles, Eric brought in renowned choreographer Arlene Phillips and a troupe of young, good-looking dancers. As well as giving the show some youthful energy they, along with filmed clips from the TV series, would give the Pythons time to rest and to change.

The show itself was imaginative and extensive. They performed some old sketches live for the first time, including "The Spanish Inquisition" and "Anne Elk"; there were more songs than usual with "The Galaxy Song" (updated to feature Professors Brian Cox and Stephen Hawking), "Every Sperm is Sacred" and "Christmas in Heaven" from *The Meaning of Life* movie all adding to the repertoire; "Blackmail" brought in a different celebrity guest each night, including Stephen Fry and Mike Myers; and there was even a dance version of "Silly Walks".

The shows were a resounding success as sell-out audiences hung on every word and joined in every sing-a-long. The press reviews were glowing and a host of younger comedians arrived to pay homage to their own idols. Still, Monty Python were not going to go quietly. The final show – on July 20, 2014, was named "The Last Night of the Pythons". It was to be broadcast live around the world on 2,000 TV channels and cinemas in over 100 countries.

As some of the show was broadcast live in the UK before 9 p.m. – the channel had a problem with some of the words of "The Penis Song". As a solution, Eric penned a piece for the channel to use to fill in while the song was performed. This would be the latest and the last-ever Python sketch; a short piece performed by a prim-and-proper middle-aged woman played pitch perfectly by Michael Palin.

As Eric, John, Michael, Terry G and Terry J took their final bows, a dedication to Graham appeared on the screen. It was followed by the simple notice: :Monty Python 1969–2014". This really was the end...

Of course, it was no such thing. The 02 Show was nominated for a BAFTA TV Award in 2015 and *Monty Python – The Meaning of Live*, the 'making of' feature, was nominated for several awards. Python went digital as their whole catalogue was re-released across all platforms, and the official website, montypython.com, continues to provide clips, merchandise, news stories and more to the global family of Python fans.

There was no way they would be allowed to slip away quietly...

"The Pythons came, they doddered, they conquered... The live material looks far more golden than olden, reminding us at every turn of the debt we owe them... The mash-up finale of Dead Parrot Sketch and Cheese Shop is worth the price of admission alone."

Dominic Cavendish, The Telegraph

"We are the only five people who know what Python really is all about, and that's quite something – it's like being keepers of some strange mystery."

Michael Palin, Time Out magazine

"Who would have though 40 years ago we would all be sitting here doing Monty Python eh?"

Python perform Four Yorkshireman at the 02

"We went on sale and suddenly we were world news. We were terribly tickled as we'd been forgotten for so many years."

John Cleese

"We'll see a proper Python reunion, just as soon as Graham Chapman comes back from the dead. We're talking to his agent about terms."

Eric, 2010

"Laughter is the fuel of the Pythons – without that they die; sad horrible old men withering away in their lonely mansions!"

Terry Gilliam

"One of the most difficult things is the quick changes. When you are over 70 there's no quick way to get your trousers on and off... This could be the Pythons' velcro night."

Michael Palin, BBC Imagine programme.

"I mean, who wants to see that again really? ... A bunch of wrinkly old men trying to relive their youth and make a load of money, I mean, the best one died years ago!"

Mick Jagger, video message to the Pythons in reaction to the reunion announcement

THE
M!